One Hundred Stories for
One Hundred Years

One Hundred Stories for One Hundred Years

A history of Wood's Homes as told by the
people who lived and worked there

Clem Martini, editor

Brush
Education Inc.

Brush Education Inc.
www.brusheducation.ca
contact@brusheducation.ca

Copy editor: Eva Radford
Cover and book design: John Luckhurst
Cover artwork: David Westelmajer, stained glass art, 2010

Printed and manufactured in Canada

Ebook edition available at Amazon, Kobo, and other e-retailers.

Library and Archives Canada Cataloguing in Publication

One hundred stories for one hundred years: a history of Wood's Homes as told by the people who lived and worked there / Clem Martini, editor.

Issued in print and electronic formats. ISBN 978-1-55059-547-5 (bound).

1. Wood's Homes (Children's mental health centre)—History—Anecdotes.
2. Wood's Homes (Children's mental health centre)—Employees—History—Anecdotes.
3. Child mental health services—Alberta—History—Anecdotes.
4. Child mental health services—Northwest Territories—History—Anecdotes.
5. Mentally ill children—Alberta—History—Anecdotes.
6. Mentally ill children—Northwest Territories—History—Anecdotes.
7. Families of the mentally ill—Alberta—History—Anecdotes.
8. Families of the mentally ill—Northwest Territories—History—Anecdotes. I. Martini, Clem, 1956-, editor of compilation

RJ502.C3O54 2013   62.2083097123   C2013-906676-4   C2013-906677-2

Produced with the assistance of the Government of Alberta, Alberta Multimedia Development Fund. We also acknowledge the financial support of the Government of Canada through the Canada Book Fund for our publishing activities.

**Government
of Alberta** ■   Canadian   Patrimoine
Heritage   canadien

Dedication

This book is dedicated to the thousands of courageous young people who sought and found help at Wood's Homes, and to the dedicated individuals who provided that help.

Contents

Preface

The "one hundred stories" concept has been developing for some time.

Jane Matheson, PhD, RSW, CEO of Wood's Homes since 1995, felt that as Wood's approached its milestone one hundredth anniversary, one way of acknowledging the many achievements of the organization would be through honouring the individuals who had been involved in its development. The best way to do that, she thought, would be through sharing their stories—one for each year of the organization's existence.

She asked if I would get involved and shepherd the project. I have an interest in stories and a long history with Wood's Homes, having run a theatre program for them for a couple of decades, so I said yes, and then embarked upon a quest to collect stories.

The task of obtaining these stories proved more difficult said than done. After all, over the space of a hundred years, people come and go. Tracking down certain individuals was challenging. Many of those who were first involved in the earlier days of Wood's Homes had passed away; those still present were sometimes uncomfortable with the notion of being interviewed. Some didn't like being put on the spot, and others couldn't remember all the important details in the moment. And of course, some events are beyond personal recollection because they happened a hundred years ago.

As a consequence, I've elected to harvest stories in the most liberal and inclusive sense of the word. Some of the stories are large and complete, while others are short but trenchant recollections. Many of the stories were related to me during interviews delivered in person or over the phone. Some were e-mailed to me, or e-mailed to Wood's Homes and forwarded to me. Some are excerpts of letters lifted from archives, or incidents drawn from articles in newspapers or newsletters. Many of the earliest are excerpted from the excellent manuscript "Children of the Storm," authored by Grace Wiwad Elsaesser. Others are distilled from working journals, end-of-year reports, letters written to catch the attention of the prime minister— and some are simply farewell messages handwritten on slips of paper and inserted under pillowcases by departing clients for the benefit of incoming clients.

In the end, the variety adds a kind of charm. The stories are by turns prosaic, touching, and comic. They offer separate points of light that, together, illuminate the organization of Wood's Homes over the breadth and length of time it has been in existence.

As one can imagine, collecting stories about an organization such as Wood's Homes raises issues of confidentiality. Names of individuals mentioned in stories have been changed in many cases. Where the individual telling the story is not credited, it is because he or she has preferred to remain anonymous, or because a source name was not attached to the original document.

I've attempted to place stories in rough chronological order, moving from the earliest moments of Wood's Homes history to the latest, although as one transitions into the later, more contemporary anecdotes I've somewhat abandoned this device. It can be challenging—and rather beside the point—to determine if a story happened a year ago, or a year and two days ago. To help readers keep things clear, two separate appendices have been provided at the conclusion of this book. The first offers a timeline of significant events as they occurred at Wood's Homes; the second offers a brief description of the programs created and offered by Wood's Homes, in the historical order in which they were generated.

Ultimately, this compilation of stories proves one thing in particular: Wood's Homes has a great deal to celebrate. A variety of stories have been shared, but all are connected by the deep love they express for the children who have been orphans, clients, and guests of Wood's. Every story is unique. Every story tells its own tale. Taken together they weave a rich tapestry. They complete a more complex and nuanced narrative that details the growth and development of an organization that has had tremendous impact upon many thousands of children and their families and, by extension, on the people of the Province of Alberta and beyond. Here are the stories of the counsellors and caregivers, clinicians, ministers, administrators, psychiatrists, psychologists, social workers, board members, children, young people, and parents, who, together, have made up Wood's Homes.

Welcome to *One Hundred Stories for One Hundred Years.*

—Clem Martini, November 2013

Reverend Wood with his large family.

Beginnings

Wood's Homes came into existence because of a tragic loss and a generous act of giving. The sudden, accidental death of Reverend Wood's wife, Ann, in Melfort, Saskatchewan, resulted in his request to be removed from his parish. This transfer was granted and Reverend Wood moved to Innisfail, Alberta. Shortly after he arrived, a soldier who was off to war approached him to ask Reverend Wood to care for his children while he was gone.

The rest, as they say, is history. Reverend Wood agreed to care for these young people, and soon he was asked to provide the same service for many other youngsters in need.

Ultimately, that first impulse to care for children proved to be the catalyst that resulted in the founding of Wood's Christian Homes.[1]

[1] In 2007 Wood's Christian Homes became Wood's Homes, to identify itself as a non-denominational organization that serves all faiths.

1

Wood's Christian Homes was founded in 1914 by Reverend George Wood (1878–1928). Wood immigrated to Canada in the early 1900s from Scotland under the auspices of the Presbyterian Church of Canada. As a young man in Scotland, Wood had worked as a supervisor of a boys' dormitory in the famous Quarriers' Orphan Home at Bridge of Weir. Undoubtedly, this is where the seeds of compassion were planted in his mind and in his heart for homeless, hapless, and harried children.

After a brief stay in Ontario, George Wood moved west, settling down in the small town of Melfort, Saskatchewan, with his young wife Ann (née Gilchrist) and their wee daughter Annie. It was here that a terrible tragedy struck the Wood family. While Reverend Wood was out ministering to some elderly people in the farming community, Mrs. Wood was lighting her lamps in the dusk of evening. Unknown to her, a careless grocer had sold her gasoline instead of coal oil, and when she set a match to the lamp, there was an explosion, and fire consumed her. A passing farmer rescued little Annie (just three years of age) from the burning house. George Wood, devastated by his loss and suffering extreme mental anguish, begged the church hierarchy for a transfer away from the scene of his wife's death and his agonizing memories. In the late summer of 1914, he was granted a transfer to Innisfail, Alberta, where the story of Wood's Christian Homes begins.

Reverend George Wood and Annie moved into a small house near the old Innisfail CPR station, and the reverend took up his assignment as minister of a new congregation. George's recently widowed mother arrived from Paisley, Scotland, to keep house for her son and motherless grandchild.

The onset of the Great War saw Canada's young men go overseas to fight for King and Country. A Mr. Porter, a young father and husband who was drafted into the army, was home on leave in Innisfail prior to embarkation when his wife died from pneumonia. The soldier, due to ship out, found himself a widower with three children. In his hour of desperation, he took the children to Reverend Wood who agreed at once to take the children under his roof and into his care. These circumstances precipitated the formation of Wood's Christian Home.

Opening of the orphanage, Innisfail, Alberta.

The Porter children were to be the first of many to come under the sheltering, ever-expanding umbrella of love and care offered by Reverend Wood and members of his family.

In the months following, Reverend Wood found himself inundated with requests to care for more children; all were accommodated, even though space and help were scarce. Granny Wood assumed the responsibilities of cooking, cleaning, and generally attending to her charges, but soon the number of children exceeded her stamina and determined efforts. George Wood realized that he would have to give up his ministry in order to devote all his time to the needs of his ever-growing "Family."

As Kerry Wood tells it, "Uncle George removed his clerical collar, tied an apron around his lean waist, and learned the mysteries of changing diapers and blowing small noses."

During this phase, George moved his charges into the old abandoned Innisfail Hospital in order to accommodate them all. George knew he would need permanent help and continual financing for his Family if he were to provide and properly care for them all.

—Grace Wiwad Elsaesser, "Children of the Storm"[1]

[1] Permission to use this story and all stories drawn from "Children of the Storm," by Grace Wiwad Elsaesser, was generously provided by the author's sons Eldon, Derek, and Scott Elsaesser.

2

No blare of trumpets inaugurated the new Home. Everything was done quietly and modestly in keeping with the humble start, but there was an excellent spirit of friendliness and comradeship displayed by the community. The church and business people showed their interest in a practical way by sending in during the forenoon donations of blankets, sheets, and pillowslips for children's beds, also linens, kitchen utensils, and stocks for the pantry shelves. These were all very much appreciated. Friends had previously donated pieces of furniture—a substantial dressing table done over in white enamel to match the cots was a gift from Knox Church Manse, Calgary.

Snow had fallen heavily and it was a biting cold New Year's Day, nevertheless a photograph was taken outside of about forty people who assembled for the opening. Inside it was cozy and warm.

Some happy speeches were made and good wishes expressed, and everything was open for the folks to have a look through before settling down for afternoon tea and good fellowship. A group of photographs were taken by Mr. Grant of Calgary, who came through for the occasion. Helen and her charges moved over that day and so became the first residents of the new Home. A good photograph enlarged and framed of Mr. Porter, father of the two motherless children, was hung above the bed of his little boy.

These were the objects of the Home drawn up:

1. To provide a home for any child requiring such.
2. To keep the family together.
3. To give a Christian training in simple Bible truths by precept and example.
4. At home boys will be educated for professions or apprenticed to trades or farming; girls trained for domestic service or at dressmaking, millinery or business course.
5. All will be taken care of until self-supporting.

—Janet Wood Crocket

3

In 1918, a grant was received from the provincial government. George was delighted to be able to pay off the debts he had incurred with the patient merchants of Innisfail. Shortly after, a suitable location for the Family was found just north of the town of Olds, Alberta, which consisted of thirty acres with several buildings on the property and was close to the CPR tracks. George had one large building moved to a better location and, with the skills acquired as an apprentice carpenter during his youth in Scotland, helped build a new dormitory. George's brother and his family were residing in Red Deer at the time, and the whole family aided in building and setting up the new premises.

By now, the organization for the care and upbringing of homeless children had an official name: Wood's Christian Homes.

By the time the Home moved to Olds, the number of resident children was nearing fifty, with the number steadily growing. Mother Wood instituted a new method of care for the children. The older children, especially the girls, helped to look after the younger ones.

The older girls also shared housecleaning chores and kitchen and laundry duties.

George Wood decided he would like to make the Home as self-supporting as possible; toward this end, he purchased a few milk cows, and some chickens and pigs, which he planned to raise for food and possibly for sale. The large acreage was very suitable for gardening, and it wasn't long before George had planted a huge garden, one that would supply the Family with vegetables for most of the winter. George believed in "people doing for themselves," and he felt that a garden provided good training for the boys in elementary farming, and the opportunity for the girls to learn preserving at the elbow of Mother Wood.

—Grace Wiwad Elsaesser, "Children of the Storm"

4

By 1926, it became evident that, once again, larger premises were needed to house the Family. On a trip to Calgary, George Wood spied a large vacant mansion on the bank of the Bow River, which piqued his interest.

This mansion, built in 1912, had been part of the original Hextall Estate, which included the area now known as Bowness Park. The Hextalls were originally from England, and their heritage was reflected in the Elizabethan-style mansion that overlooked their ranch—most of today's Bowness area.

John Hextall donated the Bowness Park site to the community on the condition that streetcar service would be provided to that area. The Seventh Day Adventists took ownership of the mansion and the property on which it was situated, sixty-six acres of beautiful woodland, just across the river from Bowness Park. When George Wood took a tour of the mansion, he decided at once that this would be the new Wood's Christian Home.

—Grace Wiwad Elsaesser, "Children of the Storm"

The Hextall Estate.

Interior of the Hextall Estate.

5

Uncle George always stayed at our home in Calgary whenever he visited the city's churches to ask for funds to run the orphanage. (He never called them orphans, by the way; they were his Big Family.)

During one of these visits, he met Miss Annie Jarvie, a friend from Scotland. Miss Jarvie had served as a social service worker in Calgary. She was staying at our place prior to returning to Scotland for more training in her profession. Miss Jarvie was fascinated by news of the home at Innisfail. My parents said it was obvious that their two houseguests were strongly attracted to each other.

However, they said their farewells at the CPR station. Uncle George went on with his fund raising and moped around our home. My mother finally suggested, "You could propose to Annie by telegram."

The message was handed to Miss Jarvie as she was climbing up the gangplank of a steamer at Montreal. She promptly turned around, returned west to marry Uncle George, and became "Mother" of the home.

When our family moved to Red Deer in 1918, there were many weeklong trips to Innisfail where my mother's cooking was much in demand. She could transform liver, then five cents a pound, and other inexpensive cuts of beef into appetizing meals, while her raisin-filled steam puddings were favourites of the children. These visits gave Grandmother Wood, Uncle George, and Aunt Annie brief respites from kitchen duties, though all four adults tended the tables at mealtimes.

A beautiful home had been built in the Bowness district of Calgary during the 1912 boom, at an original cost of over $65,000. It was offered to him for a fraction of that figure and without interest. The sum staggered him; he was used to thinking totals of a few hundred dollars and cents, not in thousands. Yet, with typical optimism, he announced, "Yes, we'll finance it with faith."

The move was made in 1926. The people of Calgary welcomed Wood's Christian Homes with marvellous enthusiasm. Many prominent citizens were immediately appointed to an expanded board of governors, and an annual city tag day to raise funds was arranged. Calgarians did everything possible to help with the transition, enjoying the happy-faced youngsters, who were delighted with their new quarters.

As one small boy exclaimed with awe: "We've come to a king's palace!"

Hextall, a wealthy Englishman in Calgary during the pre-war boom, had lavished fine craftsmanship on the three-storey Tudor-style mansion. In addition to sizeable accommodations for the dormitories, dining room, kitchen, and playroom, there was an outside building that was converted into a school for grades one to nine.

Uncle George did not long enjoy the new setting. He had been badly injured at Olds when a farmer's team bolted and dragged him a hundred yards across frozen ground. As a result of this accident, he spent months in a back cast, and from then on his health slowly worsened. He died in Calgary on November 27, 1928, his last words a plea to carry on.

My Aunt Annie continued on as matron until her death twelve years later.

—Kerry Wood

6

Editor's Note: The following excerpt is from an interview performed in August 2010 by Anne Viray with former Wood's Christian Homes resident Hilda McCartney. Hilda will have her hundredth birthday the same year that Wood's does.

HILDA: Do you know how old I am?

ANNE: 95?

HILDA: Ya, I'll be 96 in October.

ANNE: October, October what?

HILDA: October the tenth.

ANNE: Okay, October the tenth. Where were you born, Hilda?

HILDA: Liverpool, England.

ANNE: Liverpool, England? That's really far. Have you ever visited?

HILDA: Ya, we visited. My husband and I visited there once—1945, I think it was we went over there.

ANNE: Oh wow…

HILDA: But I came over here when I was nine.

ANNE: Nine?

HILDA: When I was nine years old.

ANNE: That's really young. What brought you to Wood's?

HILDA: Oh well, that's a long story. Um, my dad came out here three years before we came cause they did that in those days, you know, and when they got enough to bring their family, they brought their family! And my dad was manager of the hotel at Carmangay. You ever heard of Carmangay?

ANNE: No.

HILDA: It's down near . . . uh, Lethbridge.

ANNE: Oh right, near Lethbridge.

HILDA: Yeah, and then we went to Carmangay, and there was me and my older sister, a younger sister, and a brother, who was the youngest. Well, we'd only been there a short while when my mother got pregnant. Cause it was three or four years before we'd . . . since she'd seen her husband, since we'd seen our dad, and, of course, it took the nine months for her to complete the pregnancy and, uh, she had a girl, a baby girl and everything was fine except my mother died two weeks after, some . . . some, uh, bowel disruption due to the birth.

Yeah, you know, and then my dad, we moved from the Carmangay hotel to Trochu and was there for a while, and I remember going to school in Trochu and I was in grade six I think. Somebody, the inspector, came and gave the grade eight people a spelling test, and I don't know why but I put down the spelling too and they looked at it afterwards and everything was right so they talked very sincerely about me being promoted. But then it was near the end of the term, so they didn't do anything. Well, then we weren't there very long, anyway, we ended up going to Swalwell, that's a small town northeast of here and we weren't there very long when uh, oh! My mother died—I told you that didn't I? And then in the meantime my dad married again, yes, and then, three years after my mother died, he died! She was thirty-four and he was forty-two.

ANNE: That's so young!

HILDA: Yeah, it is young. But why I am telling you that is because… Anyway, um, uh… where was I now?

ANNE: Your father died.

HILDA: My father died, yeah, and of course we had the stepmother and she was never very nice to us. We had a terrible time and she threatened to poison us you know? So the people of the town took us away from her, yeah, and took me and my younger sister and younger brother to Wood's Homes. But my older sister stayed with friends in Swalwell.

ANNE: Right.

HILDA: Yeah, and Mrs. Wood was so nice. A person might regret going to some place like that, you know? You have to do it. But I never regretted it. She was, I dunno, she was a wonderful lady and she was so good to me. Really, I don't know why she was so good to me, she was. And she was quite a worker, my goodness. I can see her yet, in her white, uniform, the kind of things that she wore. And I said, well geez, she's a lovely lady and quite a worker you know? She wasn't very big . . . oh of course, her husband was with her. You knew that didn't you, that they started it?

ANNE: Yes, I've seen pictures and I've read . . .

HILDA: You know? Yeah . . . Anyway, her husband died shortly after I went there and her husband had a daughter, wasn't Mrs. Wood's daughter but he must've been married before and she was quite a nice gir—lady, too. But she moved to the States and got married down there. Then you know, each of us had a job out there . . . do you want to hear this or not?

ANNE: Yes I do, I do.

HILDA: Anyway, the older kids at the home, especially girls, had jobs to do, you know?

ANNE: Right, chores and stuff?

HILDA: Chores, yeah. My chore was to clean up the adults' dining room, which wasn't a bad job.

ANNE: Better than scrubbing the toilet.

(*Laughter*)

HILDA: Then I got . . . I'm trying to figure out what disease it was I got. I think I brought it with me to the Home cause I got it, my sister got it, and then two others there got it. I think I brought the disease to the Home. I didn't know it of course.

ANNE: What was it?

HILDA: Trying to think . . .

(*Laughter*)

HILDA: I think it began with *v*. You don't hear it very much now. Oh gosh, I wish I could think of it.

(*Laughter*)

ANNE: Starts with a *v*. No, that's okay.

(*Long pause*)

HILDA: Anyway, there was a plague of it here in Calgary and we couldn't go into the hospital that looks after people, things that . . . Catching things you know? So we . . . excuse me. I used to remember words and people's names and then all of a sudden poof! I guess it's age you see? So anyway, where was I?

ANNE: You brought the plague.

HILDA: Yes, and another lady came and worked at the Home. She kept us separated. Nobody else came in. They used to bring our food there and everything. Before I realized what I had, I was in a room by myself. They didn't know I had this . . . sorry I can't think of it. They didn't know then. The, the doctors said not to give me anything to eat because in those days they said starve the fever and feed the cold. So, he kept saying no, she can't have anything to eat, she's got a fever, and this went on and on and I wasn't very hefty anyway, you know? I was quite small. And I remember Mrs. Wood coming and sitting beside me one day and she said, "Hilda," she said, "I feel I can see right through you." She says, "I'm going to get you something to eat." What she meant was in spite of the doctor. So she brought me some bread and milk, you know, warmed up, and I ate it, and I don't like bread and milk normally . . . but, boy, it tasted good. And from then on I started to get better.

ANNE: Oh wow!

HILDA: But then we had to be isolated for a while because . . . so nobody else would get it, you know?

ANNE: Exactly.

HILDA: So, I was in grade seven when I went there. Just starting, you know, in early November 1929. I was in grade seven and then I went into grade eight, so I was there two years. But I was the first one ever to be sponsored to go to high school.

ANNE: Oh wow!

HILDA: Yeah . . .

ANNE: How did you find high school?

HILDA: Oh, I enjoyed it. I don't know, the time just went.

ANNE: Time flies when you're having fun.

HILDA: Well I, really, I was quite happy I was at Wood's and I never thought I would be. I felt really badly that I had to go.

ANNE: The circumstances weren't so nice going there.

HILDA: No, they weren't, but Mrs. Wood and the other lady seemed to like me too, very well. I was very fortunate. I have been all my life. I've had so many friends even while I'm in here, so many friends that are good to me.

Hilda McCartney, August 2013.

7

My mother, Esther Barber, brought my brother, Vernon Edward, and me, Joyce Elizabeth, to Wood's Christian Homes in the fall of 1947 just before school started. We met with someone on the grounds who showed us around the yard and some of the inside of the building. I remember a little girl being stung by a bee and crying and running to get something for it.

I know my mother told us what was happening, but I was still a bit puzzled when we were left alone. My brother and I had a meal in the small dining room that first day. I do not remember everything that happened, but I have a few vivid memories of certain events that are not in chronological order.

My mother was a single parent divorced from a ne'er-do-well man who never held down a job but was beloved by my grand-mother, probably because he was a preacher for a while and she was very religious.

At the Home, we were given a sort of uniform, but I only remember the ribbed cotton long stockings and the blue bloomers. The girls had straight bobbed hair with bangs, and our hair was cut regularly. One time, my aunt took me to her farm and gave me one of the first Toni home permanents. I loved my new curly hair, but as soon as I got back to the Home, it was cut off. I was disappointed.

We were given lots of rules and guidance by the administration.

My brother started grade one when he was only five years old (although he turned six that next December). I think he had a hard time of it because I would have to come to his assistance and talk to him when he cried or was hurt or being picked on. One time my brother was brought into the dining hall and spanked with a paddle in front of all those dining there. We were both mortified, and I cannot remember it ever happening again.

Grades one, two, and three were held in one room downstairs in the main building. I do not remember my grade two teacher, who apparently died in childbirth (in 1948). Grades four to six were held in a larger room in the main building, and Mrs. Farrell taught those grades. The higher grades were taught in another building at the back of the main building.

I remember winning a pair of roller skates for having good marks (I think in grade three). I remember my last grade four assignment, which was making a booklet on a topic of our choice, and I chose the polar bear. I think I did not complete it. I remember rehearsing for a skit called "Alley Oop," and I played Oola. I remember misspelling *Arctic* and *choir*. I was a chatterbox and often got strappings on my hands for talking too much.

I remember going to Miss Farrell's home as a reward for something. About four girls altogether went also. I remember we slept in a basement room and you could see the pipes for heating running along the ceiling. I liked going there. Miss Farrell wrote the following in my autograph book, which helped me feel better about myself: "Be sweet and pure as yonder star you catch the distant gleam of; For happiness is what you are and not the things you dream of."

I missed my mother a lot, and I'm sure Vernon did, too. He was so young to be by himself.

Bath night meant all the little girls would bathe en masse and wash their hair, helped by the big girls. I remember the big zinc tubs where two girls at a time could wash.

We all found gifts on Christmas morning on the foot of our beds and were so excited about that and the holiday.

We visited Bowness Park for canoeing and playing. There were replicas of dinosaurs there and a store where we could buy Macintosh Toffee—my favourite! There was also a small park at the foot of the Home property where we could swing and go on monkey bars.

In the winter we would get large pieces of brown cardboard and slide down the small hills on the property. We had a wonderful time doing that. We often explored the property at the back of the buildings where there were trees and fields. There was an old trailer back there, too.

I especially remember the meals at breakfast because the toast was always drizzled with corn syrup, and I loved sweets. At mealtimes, we were always given letters we may have received. I remember getting one from my mother and my aunt.

My brother and I were supposed to leave the Home for good at Christmas time but could not go because of sickness. I remember being very disappointed that we had to stay a few weeks longer. I was happy to be leaving because I knew we were going to a new home in Kimberley, British Columbia. Mom worked at two jobs to save enough money to move us and to pay for our stay at the Home. My mother made us a good home. For a while we lived over a café where mom worked, and eventually we moved into a small house

Wood's Homes children in adjoining playground, orphanage in background.

just outside town. She had more energy than anyone I knew and made a good life for us.

When my brother was an adult, he had problems that I think would now be called bipolar. He seemed rootless and in search of something all his life. He died of cancer at forty-five. He had a daughter, Melissah, who is well educated and now has a daughter of her own. My brother would have been so proud to see what a wonderful woman she is.

My husband and I have been married for fifty years, and we have three adult children. He was in the military, so we moved about every four years until his retirement. I was able to finish my education as an adult and have a bachelor's degree in English and a master's degree in adult education. I used to teach business subjects, including computer use. My memories of the Home are mostly fond ones, and what I learned there became the sound basis on which further learning depended.

—Joyce Ripley

8

1930

There was a lagoon down below the Home to the northeast. A couple of years after we arrived at the Home, it was decided to clear all the trees and brush around the lagoon and make a skating rink. All of the children eagerly participated. Mr. Watkins was the only male teacher at the time, and he took charge of the operation. We cut down trees, dug out shrubs, and even dug out tree stumps. Pulling out the stumps was the hardest. A rope was tied around the loosened stump and a large number of the kids would pull on the rope while others dug at the roots and chopped them off where they could. The only machinery was a plough, pulled by two horses, which was used to roughly level the area after all the trees, shrubs, etc., were removed. The project took most of the summer but that winter we had our skating rink!

—Norman Davison Casson, in "Children of the Storm" by
Grace Wiwad Elsaessen

9

1937

Dear Mother, I have just finished reading about the Home in the paper and I think everything is true. It gave me a shelter and taught me how to take care of myself, you have been more than a mother so for those who are under your loving care I send a little donation and hope though it is not much I hope it will help a little for the Home.

I am giving it to you and if you don't mind passing it to Mrs. Robertson. It's only $2.00.

Editor's note: Throughout the thirties and forties Wood's Home received donations of two dollars, five dollars, ten and fifteen dollars, as well as many gifts of food. Potatoes, flour, chickens, a half pig, a prize lamb, boxes of apples, sacks of vegetables, clothing, pillow cases, mittens, skates, a pail of candies, a bed.

10

1939

My first introduction to Wood's Christian Homes was at a Hallowe'en party put on by the two departing teachers, one of whom I was to replace as principal of the two-room school. (The two male teachers had joined the army and were leaving that weekend.) After the party I was given a quick tour of the Home. The classrooms were in the basement of the main building, under the children's dining room and the visitors' parlour. My living quarters were in the top storey of the two-storey boys' dormitory. It consisted of a small bedroom with a private bath across the hall.

I had got the job by answering an ad in the *Calgary Herald,* which had been placed by the education committee of the board of trustees for the Wood's Home. I met with the chairman of the committee and the chairman of the board, Mr. Andrew Snaddon. After we discussed what my duties would be, and salary ($900 a year as a teacher and principal, plus board and room for taking charge of the boys' dormitory), I agreed to take the job.

I moved in on Sunday and started work Monday morning. Up at 7:00 a.m., I had to make sure that all the boys in the dorm were up, washed, dressed, and off to breakfast on time. After breakfast, the boys had to return and make their own beds, and I had to check and be sure they were done correctly; if not, the bed had to be made over again. The boys were divided into work groups, and I had to make sure that each group did its job correctly and on time. The groups were: dormitory cleaning, three groups, one for the two floors and the basement; sidewalk cleaning; school rooms cleaning; pot group—cleaning the pots and pans; vegetable group—getting the vegetables ready for the cook; and the odd job group. The girls had their teams also: cleaning the dormitory, which was in the main building; kitchen group—washing dishes and helping in the kitchen; dining room group—setting and clearing the tables and serving the food in the staff dining room; upstairs group—cleaning staff quarters and halls upstairs; and laundry group—assisting the laundress. Each group rotated jobs weekly. The boys considered the pot and vegetable jobs the worst. Often, though, they got extra tidbits from the kitchen.

After inspecting the work of the boys' groups, I went to the schoolrooms and got things ready for classes. I taught grades five, six, seven, and eight. An elderly lady teacher had grades one, two, three, and four. The preschool children were looked after by two staff ladies. School started at 9:00 a.m. with recess at 10:30 and 2:15. Noon hour was from 12:00 to 1:00. Each classroom had between fifteen and forty pupils, which made them quite crowded, particularly the senior room as the passageway into the junior room had been taken off it.

I soon found that my recesses were taken up doing odd jobs such as fixing an iron, the mangle, a washing machine, a light, or something else that would not work right. Being the only man on the staff, I was handyman, disciplinarian, and settler of quarrels or disputes, even among the staff. During dinner and supper, I assisted in keeping discipline in the dining room. After school the children were free to play until supper. After supper, any who had studying to do, did so, in the dorm or classroom. Those who did not have homework could play in the yard or basement of the dorm until bedtime, which was 8:00 for the younger ones and 9:00 for the older ones. After getting ready for bed, the younger ones would gather around me on one of the beds and I would read or tell them a story. Then out would come the cod liver oil bottle and each would get a spoonful (UGH!!) and into bed they would get, hopefully for the night. The older boys, instead of getting a story, generally sat around and we would discuss any incident or problem they had or wished to talk about. I would make the rounds with the cod liver oil, pouring a spoonful into their mouths. Some of the boys did not take it so easily, and I would have to chase them around the dorm until I cornered them and poured it in. They did it mostly for fun.

During my stay at the Home, we never had less than ninety children, but only two were true orphans. The children's ages ranged from three to sixteen. Any who had finished grade eight could attend school at Bowness High School, a short distance away.

Most of my days were very busy, and very seldom did I get to bed before midnight. Due to this and the long bitterly cold winter, I contracted a chest infection. Fortunately, I was able to overcome it with medication and rest. I did not lose any time teaching but took it easier in the evenings and weekends.

—L. A. Scollon, in "Children of the Storm" by Grace Wiwad Elsaessen

11

The arrival of fall meant children took on extra jobs in addition to their regular work in the kitchen or laundry. Ted's first job was polishing the lower stairs. Marty was supposed to dust the oak room, but he wasn't much good at it. Ted also helped to move ladders for the big boys who put up storm windows. They cleaned the windowpanes by rubbing Bon Ami on the glass. After the powder dried, ghostly white, they buffed it off with newspaper. The air around the wiping boys thickened with vaporous white dust, making Ted cough. To Marty, watching from the steps, the boys looked like over-active ghosts moving through puffs of pale vapour. Over fifty wooden windows came out from storage; after finishing all the storm windows, there were vegetables to harvest. Pulling up potatoes meant lots of work. In addition to what grew on the home property, they had annual donations of farm produce from the Hutterite community, which had to be trundled into the great dank root cellar.

The Hutterites came in early October, arriving in big trucks with heaps of vegetables piled in the back. They were large solemn men, bearded, and dressed in black. The older ones sat in the cabs, while the muscular young men rode on top of the produce. These benefactors never smiled at the kids. The silent men worked steadily at unloading the bountiful harvest into barrows, which the older boys trundled away. Most of the smaller kids sat about, soberly watching the despised vegetables vanishing into the root cellar. There were immense turnips, mountains of spuds, heaps of carrots, and bulging bags of onions. The watchers' collective mood sank as the storage bins filled, the children becoming aware that they would be eating all that dreadful abundance through the coming winter. The splendid size, quality, and variety of vegetables did little to cheer them. They knew that the kitchen could transform any bountiful harvest into fibrous chunks of steamed turnip, stringy parsnip, and, most disgusting of all, half onions boiled in milk—all of it dreadful but necessarily filling stuff.

The generosity of the Hutterite community was vital, since vegetables formed the mainstay of the children's diet. They always stayed for lunch, but because of their religious convictions all things modern had to disappear. The Matron always insisted that the old Motorola radio should vanish from the staffroom.

—Francis (Frankie) Dwyer, resident at Wood's Christian Homes 1946–1957

12

It was 1940 and my parents were homesteading in rural Alberta. My father was away, training recruits for the war when my mother died, at home, at the age of twenty-nine. I was seven years old. My siblings were Ed, eleven, Nancy, ten, and Lorraine, six. With no mother to take care of us, we were sent to Wood's Home.

My siblings and I spent six months in Wood's Home orphanage. With World War II occurring, we were very fortunate to have a place like Wood's Home to go to. There were many children and adults less fortunate in other parts of the world.

A certain degree of regimentation and discipline is one of the key requirements for these facilities to operate successfully. I came to appreciate the need for this—whether by parental or other means— as I grew older. I remember that I was at the receiving end of this discipline one time during mealtime. We had to form a line at mealtime and one of the staff members noticed something about my appearance. They took me out of the line to correct the problem. This was not appreciated by me. My priority at that time was food, and the action on the part of the staff member put me at a greater distance from my meal!

Another event I remember happened on one of our nature hikes. One of the girls ran to a staff member crying and screaming as she was covered with ants. This happened at the end of the hike and staff members attended to her immediately.

One of our chores, which some of us (including me) did not look forward to, was going to the root cellar for produce, which would then have to be taken to the kitchen. Often we would see garter snakes and salamanders acting as guardians of the root cellar, along with other creatures created in a young boy's imagination!

I remember playing ball hockey on a body of water that had a thin layer of ice on top that would move or flex with our weight on it. When the staff members discovered how thin the ice was, they told us not to go on the ice without their permission, as it was very dangerous. I also remember playing rugby for the first time.

At night we went up a flight of stairs to a second floor in a long building, where we slept in bunk beds. On one occasion I recall being involved in a pillow fight. Everything was going along well until a staff member appeared and rearranged a few of us to the end of the room. This ended the fun. I could never figure out how they knew who were involved. We thought we had lots of time to play before lights out!

—Dick Moore

13

1945

Would you kindly write me advising of the procedure and steps necessary for entering an infant in your home for adoption? Also of the fees and what documents of parents, such as birth certificate, are required.

I would appreciate it greatly if you would send your answer in a plain envelope.

14

I entered the Home in January 1954 with my sister Pat. I had been an overactive child, which created difficulties for my elderly grandmother. At first, I wept many tears and spent many hours in prayer. I ran away three times because my ways were so different from the majority of residents. However, I learned to adjust and co-operate, with the help of others.

Mealtimes always started with grace. I detested breakfasts with the inevitable porridge, but I realize now that the cooks had only our best interests at heart.

We had some sneaky ways of disposing of unwanted food. One method was to scoop the food into plastic bags (concealed, of course) that we secretly transported to the garbage. Quite often, Mr. Vigas would catch someone, as he seemed to have a sixth sense where this activity was concerned.

Mrs. Birch used to scare the dickens out of me, but she made me behave. Bless Mrs. Harris! She had unlimited patience and a gift for counselling unhappy children. She made me very aware of my shortcomings.

The scenic hillsides provided many quiet hours of meditation and pleasure—I loved hiking and appreciated the beauty the Creator had provided for us.

—Sharon Reimer, in "Children of the Storm" by Grace Wiwad Elsaessen

15

I cannot forget that day in 1954 when I first approached the beautiful old Tudor-style house, perched like a pillar of strength at the end of the road. So peaceful. So welcoming. Certainly there would be many adjustments ahead, but it was much better than what I had come from.

We took pride in the Home. It was ours. The woods behind the Home were a refuge—how impressed we girls were with the forts and huts the boys built for themselves in those woods! I loved the Oak Room with its wide, curved, and polished stairway, the beautiful paneling and the elegant old organ.

Inside or out, I never felt confined, not even when there were over a hundred other children living there. Everyone belonged and everyone was equal. Nobody practiced newly learned psychology skills on us. Nobody nagged. Everyone was simply accepted. Punishments were doled out and forgotten. You never felt the staff members were keeping written files of your everyday life to demonstrate their own accomplishments. This was Home. There was no fascination with anyone's unusual or slightly tarnished background, and there was no need to talk about such things. We knew little about the backgrounds of others. It simply wasn't interesting to talk about and, anyway, we were living for today. People were accepted for what they were—no better or worse.

A sisterhood! A brotherhood—each supporting the other, all having ups and downs. Perhaps this peer group support system is what is missing in today's foster home program. The moment you move in with a "stable" family, you are not equal no matter how hard the family tries. You know that; you also know that if the going gets rough, you'll be the first one out. We didn't have that hanging over our heads—being alone in someone else's home. And where do six or more children from one family go—who would take them all at one time? I have often thought about these things. I wept when I left, knowing that I was beginning another unhappy segment of my life.

Today I look back happily on my two and a half years in the Home. It wasn't really that long before I could take control of my own life and set my own course. I don't know what would have become of me without the time spent at Wood's Home. I left knowing that I was someone of value and that could never again be taken from me.

I cannot forget the day I returned to find the Home razed to the ground. What heartless persons were responsible for this? Who removed the fine old library and the gorgeous dining room suite from the staff dining room, or the organ, or the brass plates from the doors? Where are they now? To my knowledge, there was never any consultation with anyone whose home this was or any of the supervisory staff who were close enough to understand the implications of such a catastrophic move. It left us with no place of our own, no roots to return to. No group of people could need roots and a sense of belonging more.

—Pat Reimer, in "Children of the Storm" by Grace Wiwad Elsaessen

Wood's Homes, Bowness Campus, after the demolition of the old orphanage.

16

Iwas ten years old when my older sister, Charlotte, little brother, John, and I went to live at Wood's Home. My parents were divorcing, and I guess this was the best option at the time.

Wood's Christian Home was a huge, imposing building with peaked roofs, dormer windows, a grand front door and entrance, with verandas on the east and north sides. It faced the gate with the newer, little boys' building to the northeast, the school, and the house for the teacher to the southeast. Behind to the west was the medium and older boys' building. Little, medium, and older girls lived in the main building.

Inside the main doors to the left was Miss Birch's sitting room. To the right was the office where we got our allowance (fifteen cents) every Saturday morning. It was just inside the French doors to the formal dining room. The little girls' dining room was in the east-facing veranda. The basement had a large open area, bathrooms, and showers, big girls' sitting room, and storage.

Except for the annual summer holiday, this was the first time that I had been separated from my family. I should have been devastated, but it turned out to be the most wonderful year of my childhood.

I had two great roommates, Bernice and Marjy. Bernice was tall and thin, maybe a year older than me. With blue eyes and jet-black hair cut with a bowl as most of the girls' hair was. She was an only child as far as she knew and had been there for years. She remembered her dad but not her mother. Marjy came shortly after I did, with her two little brothers. She was a big-boned blonde girl, Dutch, whose mother had died, and her father could not look after them anymore. She was a very motherly girl, always looking after her brothers. They had been living in a car before they came to the home and really appreciated the regular meals.

We did such crazy things in that place. Nancy, her little sisters, and Bernice taught me to swing on the pipes. The building was grand but old and a lot of the plumbing was visible. There were pipes in the ceiling everywhere in the basement and some on the main floor for second floor plumbing. Nancy, about eight or nine, and her little sister could go all over the basement swinging from the pipes and not touching the floor. This was very advantageous, as, if you walked on the main floor, it squeaked. This was a great way to get around after lights out. It was also neat to hang on the pipes and eavesdrop on the big girls in their sitting room talking about boys.

17

I arrived to work at Wood's Christian Homes in June 1964, at which time the concept was just starting to change—a change that would gain momentum until August 1969, and, after a brief break, continue until another change in 1974, when my association terminated.

When I arrived for work at the Home in June 1964, the super-intendent, matron, supervisors, housekeeping staff, cooks, and Frontiers Unlimited looked after the children's needs. The children were housed in the main building (which, alas, has now been razed), Robertson Cottage, and Boys' Dorm. In 1966, excitement mounted with the building of three cottages. Each cottage had house-parents, the Mother being on staff, the Father having his own daily occupation, and housed a family of eight to ten girls and boys of various ages.

In 1967, it was obvious that the provincial government was not so interested in referring "normal" youngsters to the Home's setting, but rather to somewhere they could refer youngsters for "treatment," and so a treatment director was appointed, and emotionally disturbed youngsters were admitted. By 1969, the government was referring so few youngsters that we were forced to phase out. The office and maintenance departments remained to ensure continuity of the Home.

During the ensuing months, many concepts were considered for the use of the buildings and, finally, in September 1970 the three cottages were re-opened (to which was added at a later date an off-campus residence) as a treatment centre for emotionally dis-turbed youngsters, several disciplines from the University of Calgary being involved in their welfare. This was a provincial government four-year pilot project and, once again, in September 1974, changes were made, at which time my services were terminated.

—Eileen Thornton, in "Children of the Storm" by
Grace Wiwad Elsaessen

Wood's Homes:
The Social Agency

At the turn of the twentieth century, the notion of how care should be provided for young people was changing. By the 1950s and 1960s, this change was in full swing.

The concept of an orphanage as a place that simply provided a home for those children without parents was challenged. Another form of care, founded upon a belief that the psychological well being of children was as important as food, shelter, and clothing began to emerge.

During this period, Wood's Christian Homes went through a process of transformation. It changed its name to Wood's Homes. It adopted new procedures. It acquired new land. It hired staff and developed a different approach to the treatment it offered to young people. It opened new branch offices, attracting a large and diverse clientele. There was a call to address and confront a range of social problems that, up to that time, hadn't been recognized or named: Issues relating to substance dependency. Issues of domestic violence. Sexual abuse. Issues related to the acknowledgement that a sizable population of young people were genuinely homeless. Responding to these concerns, Wood's Homes generated a new series of treatment programs: Evergreen, Habitat, Canadiana, EXIT, Phoenix, and Eastside Family Centre.

18

Wood's Homes, like every other organization and business, has been moving ahead the past few years and is endeavouring to adjust as rapidly as possible to changing needs and conditions. While we are often impatient at the delays in implementing plans, the Board of Trustees has taken no steps without thorough deliberation and planning. Since our very existence is dependent on the support received from friends of the Home, no steps may be taken without due consideration of the welfare of the children and wise and economical use of funds.

—E. E. M. Love, chairman of the board of trustees, *Wood's Christian Home Annual Report*, 1964

19

I came to work at Wood's Christian Homes in 1970. I had a bachelor's degree and was hired, very fortuitously, to work with the first team of people there who would be offering a therapeutic approach to working with disturbed teens.

It was a residential program, and I considered myself very privileged to work with that team, which was headed by Peg Peters. She organized some incredible training for this team, which involved taking seminars with Virginia Satir, who was very well known at that time for her work on systems theory. She came to Calgary and trained us. For me, that was seminal in terms of my development as a social worker. I was only twenty years old and was highly influenced by that training. We were then sent to Montreal to train with various other professionals in the field. When we returned, Wood's opened for the first time as a treatment centre. We were working with the children and their families, teaching parents to work with their kids in their homes—it was very inventive! The training was incredible.

I would have to say that while I was at Wood's I worked with some of the very best people. Ultimately I went on to work in the field of the child abuse, and specialized in sexual abuse. When I look back at my work at Wood's I recognize that many of my clients had been victims. My experience at Wood's was unforgettable.

I know Wood's has grown and developed since I was there. I've kept up with it a little bit, and I know it's become a huge organization. The thinking of the time was very innovative, very creative. We had an opportunity to do some great things. I learned how to think outside the box and was very inspired. That training stayed with me for the rest of my career. It shaped who I became.

—Francis Grunberg

20

I was on the board when we were out at Bowness, and we spent a lot of time travelling up to Edmonton, trying to get a new place. Our office was out in Bowness then, in the big old home out there. We had a lot to do with getting the money people to get the Parkdale Campus built. That's one thing we did. I was on the board when the Parkdale Campus was built.

I'm a lawyer, mostly in the oil and gas business. I first came out here from Winnipeg, and after a while two or three of us started up on the board. I had the feeling that Wood's was good and compared well to other organizations; it had a very good reputation with working with kids. We got engrossed in getting the new campus going.

As I recall, before they were getting help to get the kids looked after, if I remember this correctly, some of the kids would be taken into homes, and they had to get some places in the city that would look after the kids. It seemed to me that there was that kind of thing, and we needed to move in a new direction.

—Wallace McInnis

21

I arrived on March 5, 1979, from Winnipeg, to help Wood's Homes set up a treatment facility for adolescents. Prior to my arrival, Wood's Homes had been called Wood's Christian Homes and had been a care facility that housed children in need of foster care or temporary residence, but it had never been certified for treatment of children or adolescents. I was asked, by Dr. Tim Yates, director of

Child and Adolescent Psychiatry at the Alberta Children's Hospital, to come and help set up a treatment facility in Parkdale, which is located just below Foothills Hospital, and to help convert the orphanage in Bowness to a treatment facility as well. Collectively, these would become the new Wood's Christian Homes.

Very soon after I arrived, I met Carol who was then director of Wood's Christian Homes and really enjoyed working with her to get things under way for the changes to come. The ground had not yet been broken for the construction of the new facility, but the land had been chosen and a husband and wife team of architects chosen to design the new structure. I worked with the Macmillans on the design and they were a wonderful pair. There were very few snags in coming up with the design, and before long the construction of the new facility started.

One member on the board of directors wanted some rooms to be equipped with locks like jail cells in case some of the adolescents were dangerous or very criminal, but I refused to accept such a change and would have those adolescents sent elsewhere, if necessary. Wood's Christian Homes remained an open treatment facility.

Prior to my taking the helm of the new treatment facility, I helped Dr. Farnell run the Young Adult Program at the Foothills Hospital, which allowed me to work in my field of expertise. When I eventually came to Wood's Christian Homes, the same member on the board of directors had already chosen a psychologist to be my assistant director of clinical services as well as the person to be my business manager. I eventually replaced the business manager with a new one of my choice, Mr. Bill Roberts, and he was a delight to work with. I eventually had to let the assistant clinical director go. I was directly involved in choosing the rest of the staff, eventually totalling 150. However, because of the boom that was happening in Calgary at the time, it was necessary to go to Toronto and use our government office there to do most of our hiring.

The new Wood's Christian Homes was eventually renamed Wood's Homes. It had a voluntary board of directors; many of them were wonderful people with whom I had the good fortune to spend time, socially and professionally. Wood's Homes had been willed an operating fund by Reverend George Wood on his demise many years earlier, but it was not enough to run such a large operation, so we received funding from the provincial government. I had the opportunity on a number of occasions to deal directly with Premier Peter Lougheed. The premier was extremely supportive and very easy to work with.

Wood's Homes housed its own school on the new Montgomery Campus. The Calgary Board of Education allowed me to choose a principal to run the school. I was lucky to get someone as good as Mr. Daryl Knowler. Mr. Knowler chose his teachers and we ended up with a great combination of teachers and support staff. As an example of Mr. Knowler's innovative thinking, Wood's Homes had one of the first schools in the province to have computers for the students, among other firsts—all orchestrated by him and his very capable staff.

During the construction of Wood's Home's new campus, I had the good fortune to also work on the Family Therapy Program run by Dr. Karl Tomm at the Foothills Hospital. There I met his personal assistant, Connie MacKinnon, who retired shortly thereafter. As we were readying the new facility for occupancy, she gave me a call and offered to become my personal secretary. I accepted her offer immediately and never regretted a single second of this decision. Indeed, I have remained in contact with her to this date. She is now in her nineties and has lived on Vancouver Island since shortly after I left Wood's Home in the early 1980s. Even in her late sixties, when she came to work for me, she taught herself how to use a word processor, which was the kind of person she was throughout her life, always eager to learn.

Dr. Gerry Fewster was a PhD psychologist who was the director of Hull Homes, another treatment facility for children in south-west Calgary. We worked together on a number of occasions. We agreed that Wood's Homes would look after adolescents from age fourteen to eighteen and Hull would deal with children thirteen and younger in need of treatment. Again, it was a pleasure to have such a good relationship with Hull Homes.

In the new Wood's Homes facility we set up a number of treatment programs, ranging from individual to family therapy with very capable clinical staff. To commemorate their official launch, we had the pleasure of having Mr. Ralph Klein, then Calgary's mayor, speak at the ceremony.

The board of directors was truly a delight to work with. I especially recall a warm friendship with Sergeant John Hibbert when he served as chair of the board. Indeed, my wife and I even had the pleasure of meeting him and his wife on vacation in Hawaii on one occasion. Sergeant Hibbert was also in charge of the School Resource Officers, which was a group of individual police officers placed in various high schools throughout the city. On numerous occasions I was invited to speak at a gathering of the officers and, of course, on the topic of adolescent issues. The group was always welcoming and seemed very devoted to their jobs.

There were so many pleasures in working with the staff and clients at Wood's Homes that it is impossible to mention them all in a brief such as this, but suffice it to say that some of the greatest pleasures came from the excellent results we saw in many of the adolescents' growth toward better maturity from the treatment they received. For many years after I left Wood's Home and was in private practice, I would have surprise visits from some of the previous patients just to say "hi" and even to show me their new child, and so on. It was always so rewarding to have this occur.

I left Wood's Homes to return to private practice because I knew that psychotherapy, not administration, was my calling. I certainly never regretted the times I had at Wood's Homes because of the things I mentioned above, and many more. But nowhere in your training as physician or psychiatrist are you given the necessary training to do justice to the demands of administering a facility of this size. After I left Wood's Homes it was administered by a PhD psychologist for a while but then came under the direction of two very capable individuals, each looking after their respective areas of expertise. Mr. Bill Roberts handled the business and financial matters and Ms. Jane Matheson oversaw the management of the treatment programs. With this new structure in place, Wood's Homes was set to expand to its present very impressive size and influence in the management of adolescent treatment in Alberta.

—Dr. Brian Plowman

22

In the early 1980s, I think likely 1982–1983, I was working in the family focus program at the Parkdale Campus of Wood's Homes. I had started as a childcare worker at the Bowness Campus in 1981, which was a three-group home, basic care agency. In 1982, Parkdale Campus was created, intended to be a "high-tech" mental health adolescent residential treatment and family wellness treatment resource with strong linkages to the Young Adult (Psychiatric) Program within Foothills Hospital. In the early days, significant senior management change created some anxiety throughout the organization. The state of upset was openly discussed and clearly evident to the young people who noticed less than top-quality care, as everyone was distracted with all this drama. These young people were in a Family Focus residential treatment program because they were already upset, often as a result of conflicts in their families between adults. They often expressed their fears and insecurities aggressively to other adults, including myself and other staff, and this unstable treatment milieu magnified existing fears and lack of respect for adults generally. They often acted this out by destroying property and assaulting others. When we intervened with them, we discussed all of this and suggested that there were better ways to express their feelings about what was going on. When asked what that might be, we suggested they express themselves as other responsible adults do and let senior administration know how they felt. Well they did just that, saying that they were going on strike, made signs, and marched in front of the administration building— all very appropriate and much better than violence and property destruction. However, what we didn't know was that they were also aware that the more people that were aware the better, so they called the media, and the rest as they say is history. We became front page news, much to the embarrassment of the Wood's organization and, likely, to its government funders.

I was asked to get the young people to stop. This was done with the understanding and debriefing with them that they had accomplished what they set out to do, and now many people were watching how this was to be rectified. It was shortly after this that Dr. Philip Perry was hired. With some strong leadership and a culture of professionalism, everyone calmed down as we focused on what was the best care for the young people at Wood's Homes.

—David Horricks, MSW

23

I have now been gone from Wood's for over five years. I first began to write this several years ago after pondering that my association with Wood's represented 25 per cent of its evolution. This was a particularly significant to me considering that through my time at Wood's I was in a position to guide, shape, and perhaps obstruct its path. Now with more time lapsed and the air becoming clearer, it is time to complete these notes.

When I stepped onto the stage in 1982 there was a general understanding that Wood's had begun a new life in or around 1969 with its evolution into a group homes program. It would now be my interpretation of the past to say that, in hindsight, not that much changed until the months leading up to the opening of the Adolescent Care Centre.

As Wood's approaches its one-hundredth year and I look back at my twenty-four years, it occurred to me that I was on duty for one quarter of the time that Wood's has been attending to children's needs. Looking back at those early days of Wood's Christian Homes, and continuing on through all the experiences and conversations I have had with children in care at different points, it feels as though time were compressed.

My Introduction to Wood's Christian Homes

Only a year after arriving in Calgary, at the age of thirty-two, I responded to an advertisement by Wood's Christian Homes for a business administrator. Not yet knowing just what kind of an organization this was, and without doing any research, I prepared and mailed my application. Within days I was called and offered a time for an interview.

Having only learned that it was something to do with kids, I reported at the appointed time. I remember so clearly wanting to make a professional entrance and wondering which of the double doors was overlapping the other and should be opened first to avoid making a clattering entrance. My choice was correct and I entered without mishap, but for the next twenty-four years recalled this moment every time I used those doors!

Connie, a very professional executive secretary greeted me and, somewhat stiffly, advised me that Dr. Plowman would be with me shortly. Hmmm . . . Wood's Christian Homes . . . Dr. Plowman.

Oh great, I hadn't been in a church for anything but weddings and funerals since I was a child and in a few moments I would be interviewed by a guy with his doctorate in theology! Needless to say that any optimism I had for a successful outcome plummeted. At this early stage in my career I did not have a lot of interview experience. Up to this point I had applied for two jobs in my adult life and been hired on the first interview both times. My average was about to change, I was certain.

Moments later Connie appeared again and ushered me in to meet Dr. Brian Plowman. He was over-the-top friendly, grinning ear to ear as he introduced himself, telling me that he was an adolescent psychiatrist. Having a business background only in paint and stainless steel food systems, this information was no more comforting than my earlier worries of being even a weak participant in a conversation with a theologist. Sensing that I might not be completely at ease, Brian immediately reassured me that he realized it would be inappropriate to use psychoanalytical skills in a job interview and would not be doing so. My mental gatekeeper must have been off duty at that moment as I quickly responded, "Yes, I like to do accounting with my eyes shut as well."

All tension was gone at this point and we went on to have a very comfortable meeting. To my good fortune, Brian had brochures on his desk for Replicars, vintage sports car replications in kit form that are built on a modern Volkswagen chassis. I recognized this material right away as I had the same package on my desk at home. I inquired about his interest in them and was advised that there was a plan to build a future shop structure on site and he hoped to engage some of the kids in this as a therapeutic project. I asked if there would be an opportunity for me to participate if I was selected. The ear-to-ear grin returned. I'm certain that at this moment the job was mine. A second meeting with the chair of the personnel committee followed a few days later and I reported for work on September 23, 1982.

—Bill Roberts

24

One story I have relates to a client who was up on the roof of the school. This young person was in the Stabilization Program and he had a terminal illness. One day he climbed up there. We had to call the police and the firemen.

His therapist called me and asked, "What am I going to do?"

I said, "You have to tell him to come down."

"What good is that going to do?" she asked.

I told her, "You have to tell him like there is no choice."

So, she went out and told him, "You have to come down."

And he came down.

And then she went for a walk with him, and it occurred to her that she had a pass to the Calgary Tower. So, they went up there. From the top of the tower they had a bird's-eye view—it was an opportunity to look at the city and at his life.

He finished his time in Stabilization and went home.

You wonder sometimes if this strategy or that strategy will work, and then realize it's how you say it. In this case, it was using the resistance as a resource. Whenever a person resists, there is something special in that moment. That boy wanted attention. He wanted to get out of the prison of his thoughts at the time. And he didn't have a way of doing it. So by using a venue that was acceptable, to go up to another tower, he was able to have a look at the world, and his life and find a new perspective.

—Dr. Philip Perry

25

Before I came to Wood's Homes (I arrived from Toronto), it was in serious risk of folding. The government had put in a chunk of money to hire a psychiatrist to help kids—but it hadn't worked.

It was evident was that something was terribly wrong.

I had a deputation of kids come to my office and ask, "How are you going to provide treatment?" The kids were in charge. When we went camping, the staff would slip out to the pub for a drink.

So, we changed. We adopted a new position and made it very clear that we would never give up on a young person. In the prior operation, when the staff didn't like a kid, they kicked him or her out. Instead, we developed this byline, if you will, that stated we would never give up.

So, anytime the staff had a barn-burning kid or a violent kid or a runaway, we had to go back to the place where we started— we never gave up.

And out of that philosophy came permanent care, which was the basis of our program. Then Child Welfare began to send us all these kids who had already been given up on elsewhere.

That was in 1985.

Well, that kind of generated an attitude of covert pleasure in us. We were handling problems that others wouldn't, or couldn't, deal with. We developed an attitude that we could do something beyond merely coping with kids. Instead we cultivated an attitude that we could make a difference.

So along comes the Solicitor General, and they wanted us to provide treatment for kids who were coming out of Strathmore and other places of detention, but they could only fund it for as long as the kids were in detention—one, two, three, or six weeks. I made a decision along with the board that we would not accept funding from them any more, which was everything, half a million dollars. That was a lot at the time.

Before we made this decision, we had a look at the files, and we had a notion that underlying issues weren't being faced. Sex offences. These kids were being charged with something else. I said we're going to go fee-for-service and find a way to address their issues. That kind of creation and innovation is what we became known for. That became typical of us. And that resulted in the creation of the Phoenix Program.

—Dr. Philip Perry

26

I have many memories of Wood's. The first one that really stands out is when I was asked to do an assessment of a young adolescent. There was a question of whether or not this young fellow was suicidal, whether he was a danger to himself. So at the time I turned up, I expected to see him and expected I would talk with him. I was informed by staff that he wouldn't be coming to the session, though, so I asked where he was, and they said, "Oh, he's in a field outside."

So, I opened the door and called his name out—he didn't come. I went toward him, but he began to run away. This was in the middle of winter, so I proceeded to follow him, and during the course of me walking down long streets and crossing the frozen Bow River at one stage, I spent about an hour running and trying to interview this young chap. At the end of it, I thought anyone who had that much eager strength and diligence and could sustain his determination in that way had enough life force in him that he wasn't a risk to himself.

—Dr. Stefan Neszpor

27

I was part of a law firm whose senior partner had been on the Wood's board. I needed to do more than just law, so when the senior partner stepped down and asked if I'd be interested, I said yes, I would. I was on the Wood's board for about ten years in the 1980s and was board chair somewhere around 1990 or 1991.

A lot of change was going on. What I remember most is that the treatment philosophy was moving from a psychiatric basis to a psychological basis. That's when Jane Matheson came on board, and Dr. Philip Perry. He was the CEO. He made some dramatic changes. The thing I remember most about him was that he saw very early on that social services, like those offered by Wood's Homes, were too dependent upon government funding. He could see that there would be cutbacks, and that it would become necessary to begin weaning ourselves off of government funds and raise funds privately.

He saw that way before anyone else did, and he started Wood's on that path to self-sufficiency. I think he was very forward-looking. Very ahead of his time. I remember that very well.

That was when we experienced the serious downturns in the

economy. There was a real reining in of government funds. It was a time of tremendous uncertainty. The fear was about who would be cut first. The board hadn't done any fund raising at all. It wasn't in our mandate. We were there to keep oversight. We weren't bringing people on board to raise funds.

That has become a much bigger feature of the board since. Now you need people who are knowledgeable about certain sectors and able to raise funds if necessary.

Dr. Perry was very determined to build up the home. He was very competitive, and he saw that if Wood's were to be a survivor, they would have to do things differently.

Hard to put a finger on what exactly made Wood's different, but I think it had something to do with its ability to attract good people at the top, who were interested in staying. They attracted good people who stayed long enough to set goals and accomplish them. And they've always tried to think ahead, instead of getting caught out by events.

—Forbes Newman

28

In the mid-1980s, public interest and concern became focused on the rising incidence of adolescent drug abuse. In Alberta, two elements combined—the escalating frequency of teenage addictions and the serious lack of effective treatment programs in the province. The Alberta Alcohol and Drug Abuse Commission (AADAC) and independent social agencies were still in the very early stages of confronting the problem. As a result, many young people from Alberta were being referred to residential treatment centres in the United States. This wasn't a satisfactory approach—the treatment outcomes were erratic and the public cost was extremely high.

Three Calgary-based businessmen, Stan Grad, a rancher and oil executive, Jim Gray, an oil industry entrepreneur, and Doug Rogan, an oil company executive, became interested in this issue: What action could or should the business community take relating to this threat to Alberta youth? In particular, Stan had, as part of his expanding cattle operation, recently acquired a facility that included high-quality residential buildings. The question was raised: Might this facility be directed to some form of youth treatment? A response was uncertain. This group understood business matters but had no particular experience or knowledge of mental health treatment for young people.

At the same time, Wood's Homes was investigating the justification and limits to open a specialized substance abuse program within the Wood's complex. This independent agency had the staff and ability to deliver leading-edge work but lacked the resources to open a long-term operation.

Through separate but fortuitous circumstances, the business parties came into contact with Dr. Philip Perry, chief executive officer of Wood's Homes. This resulted in ideal circumstances— willing businesspeople motivated to form a partnership with a powerful child and family mental health agency. The Canadiana Project was under way.

Careful review confirmed that Stan's facility was not useable for multiple reasons. However, the opening of a treatment program within the existing Wood's system was feasible. Representations were made to two large Calgary-based foundations. The request was to provide start-up funding for an initial two-year period. Thereafter, the program would have to be self-sustaining.

—Sandra Snape

29

I have worked at Wood's Homes for twenty-two years now. I arrived right out of school. I completed my education and started work on a Monday. I was a brand new psychologist. I worked in a program called Evergreen.

The client's story that I remember best was Billy's. He was like a lot of the other boys: pimply-faced, troubled; he had difficulty connecting with anyone. It was really hard to know if I had any impact. I worked with him for something like a year. His wasn't a story that interested me because it was a particularly difficult one, or because he was so troubled. His story just lingered with me.

Then in 1999, there was this tall, attractive soldier at the front desk. And he said, "Hello, Susan Gardiner. You helped me." And we talked.

He said, "You said things to me that helped." He said he had a little girl now, and she was two, and he was thinking about raising his girl differently. He had spent four years in the program.

So, I guess what I take away from this is you can't always tell what impact you're having on these kids. And you can't tell how things are going to evolve over time.

Now, I don't do much frontline work. Mostly what I feel is the sense of responsibility for the long haul. What we do now will have influence on what happens in five or ten years.

—Susan Gardiner

30

I've been thinking about things. I mean I've been here twenty years—you're going to think about things.

You get a lot of feedback from clients. You get clients, who when I was twenty-four or twenty-five, they were only eight years younger than me. You get a pool of adults who call you or write to you and talk about their experience.

There's one that is, to me, a lesson about how change happens here. I thought it was interesting. It reinforced how change doesn't always happen when we think it should happen. With a lot of things we do, we wonder, have we changed things or have we helped? Sometimes it is only much later that the things we do, or the advice we give, is lived or listened to—only when the client is ready.

This was a young man who was almost fifteen when he came here, and he lived with us for about a year and a half, at the Habitat Program. Getting there . . . it takes a lot of things to happen to be referred there. It's an intensive program. Habitat, we ran it for ten years, it was a domestic violence program. It was all these boys who had a number of things in their experience. They'd all experienced violence and had themselves become perpetrators. They were getting pretty old and using violence on family. There's disruptive behaviour. It gets to the point where the parents find they are needing a lot of support.

This fellow's father had been a part of his life until he was six or seven. Both the boy and his mother would have described him as very violent. He was charged with domestic violence at the home, and that put him in prison. And that meant that by the time this young man was ten, he no longer had any contact with his father.

He saw himself as taking on his father's role, and he was almost proud of that. What got our attention was that he had threatened to hurt his mom's new baby. He had grabbed the child by his head. So that's how he came to us—in the middle of this very big crisis.

I wouldn't have thought I had a lot of hope for him. He fought treatment at every turn. His values on violence were very entrenched. I used him as training with the staff for many years. Anything he thought was unjust or unfair, he saw as an excuse to become violent. In many ways he was a very tough nut to crack.

He was into hierarchy. In some ways he saw me as a leader, but he also challenged me. Daily. I told him that violence is a trick that we get taught. One of my themes with him was how to become a courageous man. People who are courageous, I told him, don't hurt the people they love. They are able to see the impact they have and are able to put themselves in other people's shoes. We had daily groups around beliefs around violence.

Behaviourally, he seemed to improve. But we never felt that he had changed his core attitudes. He graduated and went into a group home—but we were pretty worried about him.

About five years later, we received a note from him, wondering who was still here. I think he was probably, maybe he was about twenty-one or twenty-two, and we received this note, and of course, he was told that I was still here. I called him and ended up having a couple of phone calls.

He wanted to tell us that everything that we wanted to teach him, he finally understood. When he called he was very vulnerable. He said, "Every fight we had, every time you challenged me to be a courageous man, I'm finally understanding what it meant." He is now doing very well.

The point of the story is that the way we impact people is not necessarily linear—there isn't this direct line from treatment to healing. But those experiences can result in big changes later on.

—Bjorn Johansson

31

Jade was sixteen, living on a reserve in rural Alberta. Her family relationships were very challenging, particularly with her father. Her dad's verbal and emotional abuse had taken a toll on Jade, moving her down a dark path of despair—depression, emptiness, detachment. She self-medicated to feel better. That didn't help.

Though she had some family support, even her extended family was chaotic, and she often felt lost and alone. There was one suicide attempt, and then another, and then finally, the one that would alter the course of her future: Jade tried to hang herself on a playground. It didn't work, though—she lived.

After this third desperate suicide attempt, Alberta Children's Services referred Jade to Wood's Homes Eagle Moon Lodge. Though she was nervous and initially reluctant, she agreed that the hope of helping her stabilize her life and deal with significant issues in her family was worth the effort. Reluctantly, her family agreed.

The staff was surprised when they first met Jade. She was a stunning young woman—tall, athletic, stylish. She took pride in her appearance, which was not always the case with so many youth who come to Wood's Homes. Jade was bright and articulate, but the staff learned quickly, that as young as she was, she was a tortured soul.

The staff at Eagle Moon knew that building safe, trusting, open relationships was vital to Jade's recovery. But first, they needed to do a risk assessment with her, to determine where she was at emotionally in order to help her understand her feelings and responses. Suicide was still a concern. Staff needed to know the signs to watch for, just as Jade needed to know what triggered her negative feelings and overwhelming emotional pain.

It took about three months before Jade felt more secure, and nearly that length of time for her family to engage in her treatment. As Wood's Homes is a family-centred organization, it is essential that family is involved with the youth in residence. Jade's parents had experienced the residential school system in their childhood, and trust did not come easily for them. Dad liked to be in control, and Mom was very passive, so it was a challenge to work with Jade and her workers. Wood's staff was patient though, taking the time to earn their trust, just like they did with Jade. They walked alongside the family, instead of in front or pulling them along. Eventually, the family began to work together with staff—to meet regularly, to phone conference, to share some of the challenges, concerns, and fears.

Jade continued to progress and work on her issues. With staff support she worked on the Medicine Wheel Model to achieve balance in four areas of life: physical, emotional, mental, and spiritual. She set goals under each area that included such activity as getting regular exercise and participating in recreation (she found she was amazing at basketball), understanding her emotional triggers and beliefs about herself and her family life, connecting with her spirituality by speaking with an elder and attending pow-wows, attending school regularly, and considering what kept her motivated and healthy as she moved forward. She learned about the cycle of violence and began to understand that she had choice in her life.

Through occasional home visits Jade had the opportunity to test her own strength and new skills. She learned to say no when she needed to, to remove herself to a safe place if there was chaos in the home, to communicate her feelings, and to continue to stay connected with her support system at Wood's Homes if the going got tough.

After six months, Jade attended an event with her family and never came back to Wood's Homes. Her family felt it was time for her to come home, and in the moment Jade said yes. It was nearly a year before a Wood's Homes social worker got a call from Jade. Though there had been challenges she said she was doing "okay," and that in itself was a big step. No suicide attempts. She was going to school and able to apply skills she learned to handle issues that came up. But Jade was turning eighteen, due to receive a significant cheque from the government, and she was worried about how she would handle the windfall. She had seen so many friends and family blow the money and sink deep into substance abuse.

Jade was stronger though. Wood's Homes had helped plant the seed for Jade that life could be different, that she had the ability to see beyond and could make positive choices. She knew it was time to leave home. It was not a healthy environment for her. She asked for help and received support from Wood's Homes regarding housing, finances, employment. Though Jade could have accessed housing through Wood's Homes Horizon Housing, she chose to be independent and found housing in the community. Jade found full-time work and was considering returning to school.

Through her time at Wood's Homes, Jade became connected to people who care. Lessons were taught and learned, and put into practice. Seeds were planted, and Jade continued to grow. Despite continued challenges in life, Jade became connected to her own strengths, power, and the ability to choose. Jade's life was just beginning.

32

It's early June 1989. At the time, it wasn't unusual to get a phone call from the staff at Hillhurst around 10:00 p.m. The eight young men and women who lived in that program always got up to interesting adventures in the evening. So that Tuesday night, the youth were winding down and everyone was home and settling well. Everyone, except Pete.

Always one to create exciting drama, Pete calls the group home. He phones from some undisclosed location and informs the staff that he won't be coming home tonight. He tells them that he is within a six-block radius of the home, that he is going to kill himself—and there is nothing anyone can do about it!

The staff at Hillhurst call me to let me know, and I, in turn, call my boss to let her know. We talk, and she agrees that there is not a lot to be done except wait to see what the morning will bring.

I'm still in bed the next morning when the phone rings. Pete has arrived home in the middle of the night and snuck into his bed.

I call my boss to let her know that Pete has returned, but not without some drama. As we both have our first sips of coffee for the day, our minds start churning out ideas for action—something dramatic, surprising, and unusual.

Now let me remind you this was 1989. There were few computers and the Internet was just beginning. Video cameras were the size of shoeboxes and cost astronomical prices.

And so it is with this in mind, that we concoct a plan for a dramatic intervention. My roommate and I jump into our clothes and race down to the neighbourhood 7-Eleven—they were on the new twenty-four-hour system, so it did not matter that this was before 7 a.m. They also rented video cameras.

With my newly appointed cameraman at my side, we position ourselves street-side in front of the Hillhurst Aftercare Program to shoot our new mockumentary, "Pete's Video."

"My name is Barry M," I say, facing the camera, "and I am with W double O D S News, reporting live early this morning from an ordinary yuppie street in Hillhurst. We are here this morning after reports that a young man, caught in the *grip of trouble*, very early this morning walked down this sidewalk."

The jerky hand-held camera tracks the path to the house and scans the lower bedroom window.

"Our reports tell us that this young man, caught in the *grip of trouble*, entered this window to gain access to his bedroom!"

The shot continues as we enter the house and begin to interview the inhabitants about Pete and what kind of changes are evident when he is caught in the *grip of trouble*. The staff and several of the youth are more than willing to get their moment of fame and as much camera time as possible.

"We are now," I say, "entering the room of a young man caught in the *grip of trouble*."

The bedroom door opens and the jiggly camera pans the messy room of a seventeen-year-old man-boy—only to find him sprawled across his bed, sleeping. He doesn't have a top on and on his chest is a small superficial scratch, and very carefully and artfully arranged on a white towel, is the biggest butcher knife in the house and some smudges of blood. Shades of *Psycho*!

"My name is Barry M and I am with W double O D S News," I say, "and we understand that last night you were caught in the *grip of trouble*. What is that like when *trouble* comes knocking on you door?"

"F%ck off, you guys!" he curses. "What the hell are you doing!!! I am trying to sleep . . . Hey, what's the video camera for??"

"My name is Barry M and we want to know what it is like to have *trouble* tempting you? Does it say 'Pete act like a crazy man and stay up all night and sneak in through windows . . . don't use the front door'?"

"Hey are you guys making a movie?" he asks, ignoring my question and leaping out of bed. He is totally fascinated with the camera and the art of filmmaking and absolutely thrilled to have a short film shot about him. He later spends hours watching it again and again.

That intervention seemed to have a powerful impact on him. Pete did grow up, transitioned out of Wood's and got a job—not in television news, however. The remarkable ending to this story is that after this episode, *trouble* did not come knocking on Pete's door again.

That story means a lot to me. I think back to those days at Hillhurst with so much affection. The whole environment was one of almost a kind of communal living together, particularly with the older kids, because if you didn't have a relationship, then you didn't have anything.

—Barry Mickelson

33

I thought about what story to write and what meant the most to me. I knew immediately I had to write about Lone Pipe Lodge.

I don't even know where to start in describing what we had in that program, but the first word that comes to mind is *Family*. As a group, we were family and all the children that came and went from that program were our kids. We had a strong love for everyone.

Lone Pipe Lodge was an Aboriginal program in the community. We had three strong Aboriginal staff (Tanya Sleigh, Linda Sayese, and me) and our leader was Linda Alwyn. We always said we had Linda-Say-Yes and Linda-Say-No. Linda Alwyn was Linda-Say-No, and she did say no a lot, but we loved her so much. Linda was the kind of leader who let us run the program. We set up rules, we set up groups, we set up the structure because, as staff, we were the ones who worked there and we were the ones who ran the program. Linda was an amazing leader, and what she allowed us to do gave us ownership over that program. She was positive, supportive, a mentor, a role model, and the definition of a leader. She is one of the top leaders in my life, and often, if I'm faced with a dilemma, I ask myself, "What would Linda do or want me to do."

We were tough, and when our kids acted up or struggled we were hard on them. We had a tough AWOL program and a tough detox program, and our kids didn't like it, but we didn't let up. We held them accountable, we made them attend groups, we made them go to school; we made them talk about addictions and their feelings. We also pushed them to talk about their experiences and family. People said we were being too hard on them, and maybe we were, but we weren't going to stop because our kids deserved more out of life and deserved everything we gave them.

It wasn't just all hard work. We had barbecues in the mountains most weekends, went to CBC's *North of 60* lot and got to know the security staff there. They allowed our kids to go into the lot as often as they wanted and permitted them to take pictures. We had an amazing elder who came to our home every week, and we did elder-teaching, and she even taught our kids how to cook. We had water fights in the backyard and when we were done, we would all be soaked, but man, oh man, was that fun! Our kids made Indian tacos for the agency and sold them and made enough money to go to

West Edmonton Mall for the day, and they loved going on the rides and going to the water park.

Our kids did that, not staff, but our kids.

A child learned how to wash dishes in our program. He had never washed dishes in his life and we taught him. He was so proud and he ended up washing dishes a lot after that. We had a girl graduate from grade twelve and now is studying to be a paramedic. We had a boy learn how to talk in our program. He came from Eagle Moon Lodge, and he didn't speak once while he was at Eagle Moon. He began talking in our program. Even now, I can hear him speak as I write this and it's bringing tears to my eyes.

We went through the millennium in that program, and I remember working that night and all the kids stayed awake until midnight because we thought something was going to happen, but it didn't and we were all kind of disappointed.

We smudged morning and night and set goals daily. We had amazing parties for our kids when they graduated and were ready to go home. Each one of our kids got professional pictures taken for them, and it was the first time for many of them to have such nice pictures of themselves. Even to this day, I have all the pictures of our kids. I bet if you ask the staff who used to work there or the kids who lived in that program, they will all tell you they still have everyone's pictures.

—Cheryl Bobb

34

There's a girl, a former client—she still calls me now. With her, there was major drama, incident after incident. She would be up all night just being crazy, and she would end up—she did for five years—at the hospital for an assessment for trying to kill herself. She then would check out of hospital because she had to go to work.

She was probably sixteen or seventeen. She had been through several programs, to no avail; nothing worked, she was hell-bent for leather, she was intent on hurting herself. All right, we said, we'll give it a shot. I said, we're going to move her to the Hillhurst Program, because no one else will take her and she has to grow up. She was so institutionalized; putting her in a program like Hillhurst with its level of autonomy was like . . . yikes!

But while she was in Hillhurst, the Summerstock Theatre Program hooked her like nothing else could—it saved her life. She completely bought into the program and found something in the performance. She's alive today as a result, and—something completely unexpected —finding her voice.

Since she left, I've remained in touch with her. She sounds happy, she's had her poetry published, she's connected with her family. The way she speaks, she's the strength of her family. She's living in a group home, but she's contributing. She's living a life. That's success.

—Barry Mickelson

35

A few years back, I was preparing a group for Summerstock, the theatre initiative that ran each summer at Wood's. The group was working on an exercise I had given them as research for a new script. The essential idea of Summerstock was that the kids would develop a script based upon their own experiences and strengths, and then perform it during the summer months.

A number of the kids had difficulty writing, so I would often have them paint, or make masks, or compose songs as a way of generating the initial concept for the script. In this case, as part of their home-work this time, the kids had been asked to create a clay model of the kinds of skills they possessed. Several complained bitterly but then proceeded to work. Slowly, as they shaped the wet clay, they got into it.

One fellow didn't, though. Instead, he stared blankly at the clay, then began cursing. When his profanity grew louder, I asked him what was wrong. He responded with more colourful profanity. I asked him to move away from the table and let the other guys do their work. Abruptly, he stood up, knocking over his chair. He swept a handful of the tools from the table, cursed me once again, and left for his bedroom. One of the staff tried to talk to him, but he wasn't interested in talking. The bedroom door slamming shut behind him seemed to put an end to the outburst.

Moments later we heard the startling sound of something breaking. I glanced up and was surprised to see him leaning against the front door frame, the thick protective glass of the entranceway, shattered. The arm that had punched through the pane hung by his side and was streaming blood.

When a staff member approached him, he seized a long, jagged shard of broken glass and held it in front of him. The class was quickly terminated; the other kids were escorted to the far end of the facility and locked in for their safety. The young man rushed out and loped up a hill on campus where he stopped, stood his ground with his makeshift weapon, and quietly dripped blood onto the lawn.

The police and an ambulance were summoned. We called to him, but he wouldn't reply. There seemed to be no way of repairing the class or resolving the situation, and I began to gather up the art materials. As I returned to my car, I heard my name called. I turned and was alarmed to see the young man racing toward me. I stood, frozen, and asked him what he wanted. In a quiet voice, he told me he wanted to apologize. He said he'd looked at the clay, considered his skills, and realized that he had none. "I'm empty," he told me. "I'm empty. There's nothing there." I said I was sorry he felt that way, I was certain there was something there, but he'd have to be patient. I told him that together, we could work something out. Next day, he returned to class, arm stitched up. He sat down at the table, picked up his clay, and went back to work.

—Clem Martini

36

I believe Wood's can teach the corporate world a lot of lessons. Corporations could take something away about operating efficiently and effectively, because Wood's has evolved an operating system that is outstanding. The way I got involved in Wood's holds a bit of interest, perhaps.

About 1990 or 1991, Stan Grad had a big ranching operation. It was originally a baron's property. The baron was a very powerful individual, came out west with an attitude that he would straighten these country bumpkins out, but instead he went bankrupt. Stan was a rancher, and he acquired the operation, but he didn't know what to do with these buildings that were on the land.

There wasn't much in the way of treatment here for troubled young men at the time, and we wondered if these buildings might be useful for a treatment facility. Jim Gray, another businessman I knew, and I got thinking about this. We knew something about business, but we sure as hell didn't know anything about treatment. So, I got in touch with Philip. He was most concerned with opening an addiction program, but he had no money. We rounded up a couple of the big operators in town. Well, these things all came together, and that was the beginning of the Canadiana Program.

The point being—the roundabout way of saying this—is the corporate world is often saying, "We want to help out, but we don't know how." The social agencies want to do something and they *know how*, but they don't have the money. Wood's has a pretty good model for bringing the two groups together and making good things happen.

And the whole governance structure at Wood's has evolved with a real hands-on presence that provides advice and implements it, and in so doing the board doesn't interfere.

The way things work in other places is, the operating side too often spends too much time being frightened that the board will take over. And often the governing body is so out of touch with the day-to-day operations. Wood's has constructed a bridge between the ongoing day-to-day and the governing board of directors, and they communicate back and forth very well. It's quite a remarkable model.

—Doug Rogan, long-time board member

37

My first meeting with Mandy and her mother was a disaster. I made the big mistake of asking them both what they thought was the problem in the home. Mandy called her mom some choice names. Carol cried and responded with the same insults. I left the home feeling that I had added more fuel to the fire.

The next couple of visits were just as disastrous. They didn't agree on a single thing, and I felt like a referee at a football match. On my sixth visit to the home, I asked Mandy to describe a time in her life when she had the most fun with her mother.

She replied, "I was never happy with her," and laughed.

Both her mom and I remained silent for what seemed to be an eternity. Mandy then started saying in a small, barely audible voice, "Baking, bike riding, jogging, watching movies—we used to do a lot together."

Carol replied, "Yes, we used to."

I asked, "What happened? Why did you stop doing those things?"

Mandy replied, "We stopped when she got her new boyfriend."

Carol said, "That's not true. You refused to do anything with me. You only wanted to hang out with your friends."

"I'd rather hang out with my friends than with you and that creep," Mandy replied.

"Why do you refer to your mom's boyfriend as a creep?" I asked Mandy.

She said, "I don't know," and was silent for some time.

Carol stated he seemed to like her daughter and would often bring her treats.

Mandy said, "He should stop." Mandy later revealed that Carol's boyfriend had been inappropriate with her and she didn't want to be around him.

When Mandy was asked why she did not tell anyone about this before, her answer was, "Well, Stephanie was the only person who was interested in what I had to say. Everyone else thought *I* was the problem."

Carol got rid of her boyfriend and rebuilt her relationship with her daughter. Mandy's attendance and grades improved at school. They both reported that their communication is the best it has been in a long, long time.

—Stephanie

38

I applied for a job at Wood's Homes in 1984. I was offered the job in September or so, and right after that I went to the doctor and was told I might have a brain tumour. I had been sick for some months before with a fever and general lethargy accompanied by blurry vision.

I was terrified. I had a young family, three children, was the major breadwinner at home, and now this! I felt I had to tell my new-boss-to-be, Philip, that I might not be able to show up for work on October 15 because they might just put me in the hospital if they found something.

So, I made an appointment with this person I hardly knew and went over to talk with him. Of course, I was afraid. I cried and tried to be tough. Philip must have thought I was crazy. He talked about visualizing health and all kinds of New Age things that, while comforting for a few moments, seemed impossibly naive. I thought he was weird. I went home and tried to slow my racing heartbeat.

The next day I had to go for a test, and as I was leaving, the doorbell rang and a florist delivery was for me. The card said: "Your challenge is ours." It was from Philip and Wood's Homes.

It is hard to describe the power of that card and that gesture. I did not feel I was alone. I did not feel so scared. I tried some of his ideas. I found myself repeating that little mantra days afterwards. Here it is almost thirty years ago and I still remember it like yesterday. A person I hardly knew stepped up for me and stood beside me. He did not know what I would be like or what would happen. It was a big deal.

Maybe he will read this and be reminded or surprised. I thank him today for thirty years of mentorship and friendship and for many, many things—but *this* was the best one.

—Jane Matheson

39

One kid stands out for me. Let's call him Carl.

In the early days I had a lot more to do with the kids than I do now. Now I'm more on the administrative end, but at the time I had more to do with the difficult kids, and the older kids tended to be most difficult. There was an older kid who came to Cottage Two. The description of him in the files was that he was "chronically suicidal." I didn't understand that. If you were chronically suicidal, wouldn't you be dead? But that's what it said. It turned out he was very, very smart. His mother was a sex trade worker. He didn't know where any of his family was.

For some reason I liked him. He was highly manipulative, unlike a lot of kids in residential treatment who are just acting out and aren't really interested in if you like them or not. So I would enter into banter with him where we would try to win the argument of the day. Luckily, I would win the argument most of the time.

One day he came in and was in a terrible mood. The staff was angry at him. And they would do all the wrong things. I couldn't see how they couldn't see that he was manipulating them. I remember sitting across from him in my office. He was being belligerent. He wouldn't answer. He was aloof. His hair was hanging over his face.

I said to him, "I think you have a cold. Do you have a cold?"

He looked daggers at me, narrowing his eyes, but didn't reply.

I said, "Well I think you have a cold."

He just said, "Ya?" But he looked at me like, why am I talking about this. He said, "Well I've had it for a couple of weeks."

I asked, "Are you wearing your mitts, your hat, your scarf?"

He said, "What?"

I said, "Are you wearing those things? Because your cold will get worse if you don't." He just stared at me and the meeting went on with him staring me.

A few months later he graduated. He got ready to leave. And Barry, a colleague, invited Carl and me to his place for dinner. Barry made dinner. We went over there. Barry said to him, "What was the one thing you remember about Wood's Homes?"

The moment Barry asked, I knew exactly what Carl was going to answer. He said, "It was that day that Jane asked me if I was wearing my hat, my scarf, and my gloves."

And I thought to myself, "Okay, you do all the therapeutic training in the world—and in the end *that's* what it comes down to. Simply making sure that he's wearing his scarf and hat."

I would see him periodically around the city. He ended up working oil rigs, and he would call me up to talk. But thinking back to that, I would just be amazed by the simplicity of what works to get someone to turn around. There are countless stories from other therapists who will say the same thing: someone says they changed their life, and the therapist doesn't remember at all.

That kind of thing has driven my work. The simplest things. The simplest stories.

—Jane Matheson

40

The Canadiana Centre was originally envisioned as consisting of four programs.

Two beds were to be designated for detox in the existing Stabilization Program. There was to be an Engagement-Assessment phase, housed in its own building, and then a Treatment Program in a stand-alone building. The last piece was to be two beds designated for solvent-abuse treatment in the existing Exceptional Needs Program.

I was the manager of Exceptional Needs at the time, and was only peripherally involved in Canadiana development. I found out about the two beds planned in Exceptional Needs when Dr. Philip Perry announced it at a team meeting one day. I had to appear not to look stunned. I knew virtually nothing about solvent abuse.

So, I hit the U of C library to do some research with a view to bolstering my arguments against combining the programs.

I was shocked at what I found. I'd expected to find that it wasn't prevalent. I discovered the exact opposite. There was a ton of information and a long history of abuse of solvents or related substances to get high. Documentation was largely confined to Aboriginal communities, but solvent abuse also occurred in other pockets of the population where poverty and disconnection to family, community, and societal values was rampant. However, there had also been periods in western civilization (North America) when it was a popular fad for adolescents and young adults.

All the literature suggested that it was largely unreported and was intergenerational to an extreme. Researchers and writers had seen children under the age of a year exposed to solvents (such as glue in plastic bags) by parents and other caregivers. Parents, adult caregivers and siblings modelled "using" openly in front of very young children (three to five years), and older siblings taught younger siblings the how-tos of use. According to the literature, the range of products used ranged from glue, paints, paint thinners and related products, to gasoline and indiscriminate experimenting with products individuals thought might produce the same effect.

After the solvent abuse component of Canadiana was officially launched, we added propane to the list. The staff and I deemed it as the worst, because of the rotten egg odour added to propane to identify it as a noxious substance. I can remember having to move interviews with young people who had used within the previous twenty-four-hour periods to a picnic table or doorstep outside because the smell emanating from the young person in confined quarters caused everyone else in the room to become nauseous.

I found I had an argument against putting the two beds in Exceptional Needs, but it wasn't one I had expected. I was worried about issues like dissimilarity of treatment issues and underlying causes of behaviour problems, and the negative impact addicts might have on suggestible and susceptible exceptional needs children.

Instead I found myself believing that opening the door to solvent-abuse treatment publicly was more likely to result in a full house (six to eight beds) and a constant stream of referrals as word got around. Before I could even make my pitch to Philip formally, I found myself the new manager of Canadiana.

—Sandra Snape

41

I was responsible for a program called A'sokina, which had many, many Native children from all over Canada.

Christine, one of the workers in the program, was totally exhausted, and I took her to The Keg for a break. We're having lunch, we're chatting, we're relaxing. All of sudden we get interrupted and are told that we have to come to the program immediately.

We rush back—and there's total chaos. Some of the staff are crying, some of the kids are looking shocked, and I'm not sure what's going on. I feel my anxiety levels rising. Jane takes me into the laundry room with Bill and Sue, shuts the door, and tells me that one of my kids tried to hang himself.

Two of my staff ended up resuscitating him, the ambulance had already showed up, and he was on the way to the hospital. He was going to be okay. This was a very special kid. He was a tyrant, but he was special.

And so, I'm listening to Jane, not really registering it, and she's saying, "Are you okay? I know how upset the kids are, but are *you* okay?"

For a few minutes she took care of me. And after, I said, "Okay, now I can go out there."

And for the rest of the day we took care of everybody. But that's a good example of how when a crisis like this happens, nobody points fingers. That's what makes us unique.

—Teri Basi

42

Larry and Ian were two kids who were devoted to glue sniffing. We decided to take them off-campus and take them camping, so we set up this elaborate trip way into the Kananaskis, hours away from anything. So, away they went. But while they were there the kids ran away. And they weren't wearing any clothes.

Nobody could find them. Everyone looked and looked and looked. The RCMP were called; they couldn't find them.

So I went up. I said, "We're going to find them."

We went to the camp where they'd been. The staff said there had been some things stolen the night before. So then we went looking again, and this time we came across a little hut and noticed that a window was broken, and things were moved around.

So I called the park rangers and we looked around some more— still nothing. I said, "They can't be far away."

And then suddenly, I went, "Sh. Just listen."

Eventually we started to hear sounds. And we saw them and began to run after them.

I thought, maybe they can't imagine that there would be people from Calgary looking for them. So I called, "Ian!" and he just froze, like a deer in the headlights. And we got them back.

For me, this story is about perseverance. That's us. We're never going to give up.

—Bjorn Johansson

43

The death and rebirth of the Phoenix Program was probably the story I was most involved with, and it's a story that means a lot to Wood's Homes.

What happened was, I had moved over to the Bowness Campus. That was in 1985, and at that time Cottage One was for the at-risk kids. Remember, they used to have open custody. The kids were charged with one thing or another, and because of that, there was a bit of opportunity to do a little treatment.

Anyway the kids we got were the at-risk kids; in essence, they were at-risk in a closed setting. They were little kids with big mouths.

They would say the wrong thing to a big kid and get pummelled. Top of the list of these at-riskers were the ones called "skinners"— the kids with sex offences.

At the time Gary Sanders was the psychiatrist involved. He would come to us and he would say, "Why don't we make a designated group for sex offenders? The literature says it might be a good idea."

Philip Perry was there at the time and he was good at new and novel ideas, and we had Jane on staff and she was very good at autonomy and self-direction. So, with them you had an opportunity. If you thought you had a good idea, you would be permitted to pursue it. It wasn't a free-for-all—you had to do your homework first.

So we wrote a proposal to the Solicitor General in 1988. We got some funding and Phoenix, a program for teen sex offenders, got started. Dr. Sanders got involved. People would call us to see if we could take their kids, and if we had a bed free, we would take them.

Then, one cold and blustery day in 1990, Jane found me in a bar after work. She told me that the Solicitor General was cancelling the funding for the program. We had two months' notice, and they wanted it closed by then. Philip and Jane had discussed these matters and said to me, "We can close it down, and we'll find a position for you or, we can go completely fee for service—but in six months it's got to be entirely self-sufficient." I chose the latter.

We always had a kind of tough relationship with the Solicitor General back then, because for them everything was black and white, right or wrong, and Wood's has nothing black and white about it. So, we held a party that was a wake for the Solicitor General. Everyone had to come in black and white. We burned her in effigy. It was about us taking charge.

That was a rallying party for the staff—and nobody left. Nobody thought, oh my god, we lost . . . how many thousands of dollars have we lost? We just started raising money.

Philip was a real stickler for getting things right. My wife's sister was a design person, and she made a logo, and with it we made this brochure. Within four months the program was still open, and we were making money. We've been pretty consistent ever since. We've had no issues with the kids in the community. It's been strictly for kids who are sexually intrusive—and working with kids there's a genuine opportunity for change.

I don't know if there is another program like it in the country.

Eventually this building would house the Phoenix Program.

There are other programs that treat sex offenders. There are a few programs that have tried to do this. I don't know of any that have actually been successful.

—Peter Wittig

44

The Adolescent Care Centre (ACC) was built for Wood's use on provincial land. Wood's had only to provide for caretaking activities as all maintenance work was done by Alberta Public Works, working from their neighbouring maintenance facility. The site was chosen due to its proximity with the Foothills Hospital and its Young Adult Mental Health Program. The Parkdale community wasn't pleased, initially, to have us as neighbours, and issues around traffic, parking, and access routes prevailed for many years.

The ACC School was built with a large adjoining blacktop playing surface, unmarked and unfenced and, consequently, little used. It seemed obvious to me that this ought to be a tennis court. With surplus funds remaining in the contract budget for the site, I proceeded to put high chain-link fencing, posts, nets, a practice wall, and court markings in place. I was feeling quite satisfied with my surely valuable addition to the facility when Peter Addison felt compelled to comment. "Tell me, how many troubled teens have you known to play tennis?" he asked. A few quick alterations and it was a multipurpose playing area with basketball hoops and provisions for volleyball nets.

The following year a similar project was undertaken at Bowness where recreation facilities were conspicuously absent, at least from my perspective. Immediately east of the three cottages there were overgrown foundations laid twenty years earlier for two additional cottages. The hillside down to the parking area was steep and unkempt. This hillside was bulldozed to a gentler slope and the fill used to cover the old foundations and create a level playing surface for another multipurpose court.

The Enviros Program had long been a tenant in the Robertson Cottage up until about 1985 when Wood's received new funding from the Solicitor General for a young offender program, the Community Re-Entry Centre. The building was largely gutted and rebuilt in preparation for this program.

—Bill Roberts

45

When we were running an addictions program for Aboriginal youth, the media was talking about Davis Inlet. We got all these kids, mostly from Labrador at the time. And these young waifs showed up, and yes, they were sniffing gas, but there were all kinds of other issues. One kid had his intestine wrapped up inside, and he was sniffing because of the pain.

They were really gentle, gentle souls.

One young boy was hallucinating about his grandfather who had taught him about the drum. We slowly introduced elements of his culture back to him. He was into drumming.

Then we got his mom to fly down. She walked in, saw him drumming, and burst into tears. She said, "I didn't think I would live to see my son drum again. You have brought him back to me."

She went to her suitcase and she came back with a gift. "I have brought this," she said, "to thank you for bringing my son back." It was a dead goose.

She laughed as she looked at my expression. She said, "I'm thinking you don't know how to clean and cook a goose."

So, she cleaned it, she cooked it up and made us a traditional dinner. And it was phenomenal! It was a tearful moment, and it was funny at the same time.

I don't know how she got it through the airport.

—Teri Basi

46

New Horizon was what we wanted to call our new programming idea—if it ever got off the ground, that is. It was still just a dream.

We wanted to offer "housing first" services to young people over eighteen who were having trouble getting a leg up on the future. Many of these kids were homeless, abandoned, or escaping from families and systems and generally operating with a two steps forward and three steps back routine. We thought that apartments altogether in one building would be best—not too many together but enough so that our support staff would not need to drive all around town to see their clients.

We originally wanted to buy a building, but first, they were too expensive, and second, we had board members saying, "Wood's is not in the real estate business, Jane." We happened upon a possible partnership with Horizon Housing, but it was not yet determined how and even if it would work.

So, we had this idea, but no firm building, and a gala coming up—a yearly gala dinner that was always looking for a new project that donors might get excited about.

Madelyn and I decided that a real housing first philosophy for kids would be making sure they had furniture to live with—their own. It is one thing to have a roof over your head and another to have your own furniture, which you are more likely to take care of and take when you move out. We made a list of things a person would need and came up with $5,000 as a figure. For $5,000 we could easily outfit an apartment—stem to stern. Donors felt this was a good idea, too, because twenty-five people donated $5,000, and we had enough resources for twenty-five young people to furnish an apartment. We just had to make sure we got the program now!

We did, and now we have twelve young people living in apartments at any one time. Some of them are very house proud. One young man sets his apartment up so that it looks like a show home—right down to place settings ready on the table.

Then there are others, like Lily. She left with her furniture in the middle of the night—took it all to her boyfriend's place. She had only been in the program for a couple of weeks! Luckily, we knew her probation officer, who told her to either get back to the program with the furniture or give the furniture back. She did the latter. One important point of note: her worker said to us (and rightly so), "I thought you said it was her furniture to keep?"

"Aha," we said. "We probably need to make sure there is a clause that says you have to stay in the program for a certain amount of time before it is actually *yours*!"

Now, clients need to stay for at least six months. Thanks, Lily, for this very important lesson!

—Jane Matheson and Madelyn McDonald

47

I was there from the time when I was fourteen to nineteen. I was at Hillhurst and Altadore.

What I remember is my worker taking me out for my birthday to Fortress Mountain. It was just me and him. We got up at the crack of dawn, drove out to the mountain. It was a special time. I got out of the group home, hanging out with eight other kids. Normally they just give you a cake, sing "Happy Birthday," that's it. This was special—he spent his own money skiing with me.

Another worker, a female staff, took me home for Christmas once, because I had nowhere else to go.

48

When I arrived, the province was in the process of assembling land around the city for a transportation and utility corridor, known as TUC. They had been in negotiations with the Wood's board for a number of years already seeking to purchase much of our Bowness backyard. I thought of the Bowness site in two sections, a seven-acre, almost-square area upon which all of the development sits, and a twenty-five-acre strip of land running west through to the old Happy Valley fence line, which is west of the new Stoney Trail and under the power lines, for a total of approximately thirty-two acres. Sorry, the ability to convert to hectares escapes me.

There were two primary issues that contributed to these negotiations dragging on for another ten years. Primarily, the land in question was covered with Douglas fir, many of these large trees being hundreds of years old. This was one of only two remaining stands in the city. The second issue was one of economics. The land borders Bowness Park and the Bow River, and slopes steeply to the water. Although it would seem valuable to the eye, it was for the most part undevelopable and therefore of minimal monetary value, leaving Wood's little incentive to give up its land.

It was Vern Collins, a past board member and one of the kids who once played in Wood's backyard, who first approached the Provincial Historical Resources Board seeking to have the Douglas firs designated as a provincial historic resource and thus to block them from being cleared for the Stoney Trail right of way. By this time,

Preserved glade of Douglas firs to the west of the Bowness campus.

Alberta Transportation had its sights on all of the land up to just west of Cottage One, almost all of the twenty-five-acre strip. In time the Historic Resources Board agreed with Vern, and it was time for the Wood's board to make the decision to formally ask for this designation. To be sure that the issue was fully appreciated by all present, the board committee meeting was called to be held in the clearing just to the west of the trees known to Vern and childhood friends as the Three Sisters, under the umbrella of the most majestic trees. The maintenance staff brought out a table, coffee and donuts were served, and the board members had no difficulty in agreeing that this area must be preserved.

To hold the TUC purchase to a minimum and yet retain a remote chance for future buildings to the west of Cottage One, the historic designation was requested for only the land upon which most of the major trees were rooted. This was from the point that drainage or spring water crosses the path to the west up to all but the most easterly three-and-a-bit acres. The Douglas Fir Tree Sanctuary designation was made as requested, and permanent signs were erected at both entry points, welcoming the public and letting them know that this designation was at Wood's initiative.

Alberta Transportation now had no choice but to negotiate only for the unprotected land, creating a bottleneck in the TUC. This now meant that much more land had been acquired for the TUC before and after it crossed Wood's land than could ever be utilized for that purpose. Wood's was then able to trade the just-over-three acres for flat marketable land to the south. This land was subsequently sold to a developer and proceeds, about $120,000, placed in Wood's endowment.

—Bill Roberts

49

This used to Be
my Bedroom. At
woods it is a
Safe place to talk
about feeling. talk
aBout what happ-
end iA the past.
and Hord things.
and You are
not Hear Becouse
you Have Been
a Bad boy or gal you
are hear to get
Your Heart healed

from Justin

50

This is a story that involves program managers, dedicated staff, and an extremely troubled young girl. This young girl came to Wood's with a tragic story behind her. She was young, raised by her mother and grandmother in British Columbia. She was born with fetal alcohol syndrome disorder (FASD) and was introduced to crack cocaine by her mother and grandmother at twelve. Not long after that she was introduced to the sex trade. She contracted hepatitis C and became malnourished. She had a history of criminal charges related to prostitution, violence, and theft, and struggled to fully comprehend what was occurring to her and around her. The authorities in BC had decided that, despite her numerous charges, they were going to send her to Wood's in an attempt to have her enter treatment and make some changes in her life versus going to jail.

When she arrived at the Stabilization Program, she was extremely underweight, dressed in a tiny top and even tinier skirt. Some staff were worried about having a potentially violent youngster with hep C in the cottage. The manager at the time, Ryan Clements, was determined to give this girl a chance. He made sure that she arrived safely at Cottage C and made good plans with the staff to develop a plan that could not only meet her severe attachment needs, but also her withdrawal from drugs. He even went shopping at Wal-Mart to buy a change of clothing for her (even though she didn't love Ryan's taste).

The young girl struggled with the routine and structure of the cottage. There were times she would run back to her perception of the safety of the streets. After a few weeks she transferred from Stabilization to Cottage D. One of the first things that happened was that they took her camping! They gave her her own tent so that she had privacy. They understood that the withdrawals kept her up at night and that being in the wilderness would put her out of her comfort zone. I would never say that the trip was perfect, but wow! She took risks just being there. She even went on the zip line (picture it—in a miniskirt and heavy makeup). This young girl's story ended, unfortunately, with her returning to BC to complete her jail time, having found the lure of the streets to be too much for her to handle here in Calgary. But during her intake process and her stay, we learned a lesson from Ryan about never saying no.

—Susan Ward

51

I was working late one night, minding my own business, and suddenly I heard screams of what sounded to be a child. The child was screaming, "No, no, no!"

I thought, "We don't have a dentist on site, so that can't be what it's about. And the nurse had gone home, so it can't be someone getting an injection."

I knew this wasn't an expression of annoyance. It was something much deeper. Anyway, I was to find out later that it was this was young fellow who had been dropped off at Wood's. His mother had brought him, and it turned out she was going to leave him. She didn't want him anymore.

I realized something then. I'd thought that these were difficult kids, kids in crisis, that they were "bad" in some way, I suppose. It took that episode to make me realize the kinds of situations that arise, and I came away with a totally different perspective. It made me realize that, for whatever reason, this mother was giving up her child, and it was difficult, and it made me reflect on our mission statement. And it made me think about persistence.

—Bruce Monnery, a director of finance

52

Billy and his mother struggled for years to maintain a relationship with one another. Billy was an eight-year-old boy with a three-year-old sister. Billy's mother struggled with depression and often found it hard to find the energy to engage with her two children who had lots of energy. When services commenced, Mom expressed that she would like to improve her relationship with her son but was not sure how. Through observation of their interactions, the writer was able to develop a plan with Billy's mom based on Billy's needs, which would at the same time benefit her.

The writer observed that Billy often wished to play with his mom and have her do activities with him or at least give him permission to engage in activities. His mom often said no or told him to go play by himself or with his sister and she would watch. Billy's disappointment was evident; playing with his sister often resulted in a dispute and Billy getting in trouble with his mom.

The writer brought in the method of teaching the mom how to be an active parent. This was difficult without her seeing a doctor at Alberta Mental Health regularly to deal with her depression, so we first addressed this, and she now sees a doctor every other week. In teaching her active parenting techniques, it was important for this mother to understand how they would benefit her. For instance, she came to understand that if she had an activity ready for when Billy came home he would spend some of his energy on the activity as opposed to quarrelling with his sister, which would force her to respond. The writer sat down with the family and made a list of after-school activities they would both like to do. Billy's mom was quick to point out reasons why some of the activities could not work, but when reminded how it would benefit her she decided it was okay to try.

With the help of the writer she enrolled Billy in Cubs. The writer stressed to her every week the importance of her getting him there and also working on badges at home because it is something he enjoys and wishes to excel at. Now, there is no need to stress the importance, she has grasped it. She says, "We have become closer to each other. I now know what he needs and he seems easier to manage now that we do things together."

53

I came up from the United States and, at the time, there was this whole notion that there were no homeless kids in Calgary. And I thought "Well, good for you, if you've solved this problem." And so, I returned to New York.

Then I got a call from Calgary, and I was asked to come back and actually count the number of homeless kids. What we discovered was that kids were running from the child welfare system. We counted over four hundred kids—but the aldermen kept saying there were no homeless kids.

We said, "Our research tells us you have kids living on the street or moving from place to place trying to survive. Don't you want to put some money together to help them?"

I got invited to initiate something (I had worked on a shelter project in New York). But then they felt if they were going to put their money into anything, it would be this whole war on drugs thing, so suddenly the money disappeared.

Sue Fordyce and Madelyn McDonald accept a cheque on behalf of EXIT.

By the time I got to working with Wood's Homes, the number of homeless kids was growing. So the Government of Alberta put out a call for proposals. We put a proposal together and this time it was accepted, so we had to find a location. EXIT (our new program) needed to find a home. We finally found one on 16th Avenue NE. Then I helped with the shelter down in Lethbridge. The shelter in Lethbridge is the same physical layout as the one in Calgary. Many people see homeless shelters like, "Oh my god, why would you put them in a shelter, why not a long-term facility?"

My opinion is that it's important to get homeless and troubled kids into a safe place quickly. Kids were running and winding up dead. They were being killed. Many were running from some very horrible situations, only to encounter some other, unexpected, horrible situations. Shelters were a safe place to go.

The reality is we've got more young people with no place to go than we have places to live.

—Madelyn McDonald

54

This is a story about a young man who really worked at things, coming full circle in his life. He was born with suspected FASD. He lived with his dad for many years until his behaviours became too hard to handle. This meant that Child Welfare became involved. Because his behaviours continued to escalate, it was decided that he would need residential care. In fact he was one of the original U12 (under-twelve) kids (way before the program was called U12). After U12 this boy moved to other placements and ended up being placed at a community program in a teaching home.

His behaviours became harder to support as he got older. The program he was in was going camping, but the staff decided that his behaviours were too high-risk to take him along. The program staff asked Placement to find an alternative residence for him while they went camping. Placement found him a ten-day stay at Catalyst. The day after he landed at Catalyst, the staff packed him in a van and took him camping for four days! And he did fine!

This young man ended up staying at the Catalyst Program for a year. Eventually, he left on a successful note, moving to the Altadore Program. Before he left the Catalyst Program, he called U12 to ask if they had any projects he could work on for his community service hours. They did, and he went up and assisted with the re-organization and cleaning of their storage room. In fact, this young man pointed out to the staff assisting him that the materials he was cleaning up were, in fact, materials he had broken years earlier when he had resided there. He pointed out that it made sense for him to be cleaning it up, even if it was years later. This young man went on to be a volunteer firefighter and eventually moved from the Altadore Program to an independent living program.

—Susan Ward

55

It was my first month on the job and time for me to go out to a family visit with a more experienced staff member.

I had no idea what to expect in this home, aside from the file set-up that we had done over the phone with the mother. The client was having troubles with her fourteen-year-old daughter, who wasn't obeying household rules, was running from the home, and engaging in high-risk behaviours. This led to constant conflict between the mother and daughter, often escalating into prolonged yelling matches and, at times, physical altercations between them. Our goal was to meet with them, assess the situation, offer suggestions around conflict management, create a safety plan, and provide referrals for programming that could further support the family in the long run.

Upon arriving at the home, I quickly realized that the issues were systemic in nature and had been ongoing for quite some time. The family had moved here from Edmonton due to fears that the children's father would come after them. He had been in jail and was en route to being released. They had no family in the city, so immediate support and respite were not options for the mother. The home was cluttered with random pieces of this family's life. Room to sit was limited; we conducted the visit in the small living space with the smell of stale cigarette smoke in the air.

Along with the mother's social isolation from family and friends, she was struggling to make ends meet financially and was fearful of her ex-partner threatening their well-being. Add to this a young person wanting to seek independence and challenge her mother on a daily basis, and the situation had become increasingly concerning.

The mother didn't have the necessary tools to manage her teenage daughter's behaviours.

What struck me most throughout the visit was a small four-year old girl who played with her toys and remained quiet for the majority of the time we were there. At one point, she hopped up on my co-worker's lap and nestled in for a hug. I was shocked at this display and how comfortable she was with a stranger. My second thought was the reality that she might be experiencing neglect and that the constant nature of the conflict between her mother and older sister was trickling down to her well-being. She wanted comfort and stability, something that was not currently being offered at home. My co-worker and I remained focused and progressed through our objectives for the visit: assess the situation, provide suggestions for conflict management, create a safety plan, and offer information regarding programming for long-term supports. As we prepared to leave the home, the four-year old tapped my leg and signalled for a hug goodbye. I obliged this request and while kneeling down to her level to give her a hug, she whispered into my ear, "I wish you were my daddy."

That was something I didn't expect.

It's two years later, and these six words still resonate in my mind every day I go to work. We have not had contact with the family since the visit. My hopes are that they are doing well and have been able to move forward. We see both positive and negative outcomes with the families we work with—that's the nature and reality of this line of work.

We would all burn out quickly if we thought we could save the world. What keeps me going is the idea that we put our best efforts forward to support the family in a way that is accessible, non-judgmental, and we meet them at their level. Contact is made with thousands of families every year, but the focus always remains one family at a time.

56

Editor's Note: The following three stories are related, in that they share perspectives on an event that changed the way things operated at Wood's Homes.

56a

Laura was a high-spirited young woman who came to Wood's. I was the intake co-ordinator at that time and the senior therapist. Her parents called and were very concerned about her. She was the kind of kid everyone enjoyed, but at the same time could make you crazy. She attracted kids around her. When she was at the Parkdale Campus she would stir things up, and then when she was at Bowness Campus she would stir things up there. Though she was a ward of the court, her family was very involved and very concerned about her.

I became her therapist. She was always teetering on the edge of things, but there was never any clarity about what was up with her. One minute she was doing really well in school, and then suddenly she would be getting everyone going at the cottage and encouraging kids to lock the doors on staff. Her behaviour became more and more worrisome. We wondered if perhaps there was some kind of disorder and had her assessed—but nothing. She started to drift further and further away from Wood's and began spending time downtown. At first she was just on the fringe of things, and then she was in the sex trade. But, she would always come back to Wood's.

There were always people who were trying to find out what the thing was about her that made her push the envelope. And it was especially difficult, because everyone really liked this kid. Even the youth court judges liked her. People became more and more concerned.

I thought, we have to try something really different with her. So we created this character, Miss Adventure. The idea of Miss Adventure was that it was a tool for talking about what would come over Laura. And it was a way of talking about that behaviour separately—it meant that Miss Adventure was the bad one, not Laura.

Laura always had an edge. There was a time when she ate nails, for instance. Another time, I remember going to a huge conference downtown and seeing her on the floor of the building, exhausted, and sleeping—it was the building where her mom worked. Then Laura would come back and say, "I'm not going to do this anymore." So we would take her Miss Adventure's clothes out and bury them.

She would often come to my office with a knapsack on her back. I would have to look in it. Sometimes there was a cat; sometimes there was a dog. There were rabbits sometimes. Harold, who was in charge of maintenance, built a pen for the rabbits because Laura would always come back for the rabbits.

This was a difficult time for the staff. Laura knew that she was at risk. She knew that.

And then Miss Adventure disappeared for a long time. She was at CYOC (Calgary Young Offender Centre) for a while, but she would still communicate with people at Wood's, phone them, connect with them. She was released from CYOC to a group home, and there was some trouble. While she was at this particular group home, she was supposed to be there at eleven, and she wasn't one evening, so they locked her out. She headed downtown and was murdered that night.

Everyone was devastated. The funeral was a big event. Many, many people were there, including many of the people she knew from the street. The hardest lunch I ever had was with her mother after that. She asked me if Laura knew this could happen. And I said yes.

The events leading to her death broke a lot of barriers. They forced people to look at street kids in the sex trade differently. The events were instrumental in the development of EXIT, because if EXIT had been there, we could have got her safe. For a long time her mother sat on the advisory committee.

A marker devoted to Miss Adventure was placed out in the woods west of the Bowness Campus. As far as I know, it is still there today.

—Dr. Sue McIntyre

56b

Her name was Laura, and she represented a turning point in our organization.

The Evergreen Program was called Permanent Care at the time. And there was a girl in that program who was dressing up and going downtown. She was actively going off to prostitute. No amount of talking or trying to convince her otherwise worked—she was really

The marker dedicated to Miss Adventure.

difficult. She was going to do it any way, no matter what. As soon as she got beyond the eyes of staff, she'd pull out the high heels.

Sue McIntyre developed a kind of term for this: Miss Adventure. She recognized the allure downtown could have for kids—and the risk. Sue worked closely with Laura, and she was one of the strongest therapists we had—you couldn't ask for better. She was a national expert in this area, and even the best of us—Sue loved this girl, and Laura knew this—and even the best of us couldn't change the tide.

It tormented the staff. They couldn't stand it. They couldn't stand seeing this happen. Sometimes staff would go out and search for her, and try to convince her to come back. Sometimes she could be found. Sometimes not. Sometimes she would be convinced. Sometimes not. This was a very high-stakes adventure.

Ultimately things ended tragically. She was killed, her body was found in a frozen place. The whole organization could hardly take it, there was so much pain. That incident inspired EXIT. It forced us to ask, "Why aren't we downtown helping those kids?" We talked to aldermen downtown and we raised money.

During the 1980s and 1990s young girls were murdered more often in the downtown area—that happens less today. Today, I think there is a different societal acceptance of this kind of event. Those young girls aren't there for the taking in the same way they once were.

—Susan Gardiner

56c

During my time at Wood's Homes—almost thirty years—there have been six times when our collective response to very serious events of a common nature was challenged. Each of these involved being afraid, being terribly sad, being responsible, and a death.

A twelve year old came to live with us who had shot his nine-year-old sister. His family and community disowned him. He lived with us until he was eighteen.

A seventeen year old who used to live with us killed a man in a downtown hotel room, then came to the Bowness Campus hoping to find a previously employed staff person to talk to and tell. He went to prison for a long time.

A seventeen-year-old girl who also lived at Wood's Homes previously was murdered—just a day after she had been in touch with us to tell us how well she was doing.

A girl we hardly knew came to one of our foster homes and died in the night.

An eleven year old who was struggling with solvent abuse tried to hang himself with a hanger in his bedroom and, thankfully, survived.

A boy attending one of our schools killed himself because he was being bullied. He called out for help on Facebook, but no one came.

Each of these wonderful children was cared for by Wood's Homes, perhaps by just one person or by many, and their loss was felt acutely. Each member of the staff team has to manage their own upset—often in short order, as there are families to support through their grief. There are questions to be answered. We attend funerals. We decide whether to create new programs in memory of that child or teen.

Wood's Homes also feels responsible when these events occur. Why? Why not try to absolve oneself of this? Because never giving up, never turning anyone away, and never saying no to anyone who needs help carries with it a powerful sense of responsibility that everyone who works there carries around with them each and every day. Sometimes it can feel like a burden. Mostly it is a powerful force—one that ensures we remain vigilant, that we take the job of caring seriously, that we are focused on quality care, and that we also take time to take care of ourselves and each other. It's the business of helping people live a life.

—Jane Matheson

57

According to my records, it was the mid-1990s. I recently had developed an Ethics Training Program and was looking for organizations that might be interested in trying it on. I knew two people in Calgary involved in the non-profit service community and they invited me up to do the program. Somehow—I don't remember how—I got scheduled to do the program for Wood's Homes. As I remember it, we met in a basement. It wasn't literally a basement but rather an interior room of one of Calgary's large downtown office buildings. No windows, maybe forty or so participants, a day-long workshop.

Later, Jane Matheson, the relatively new (at that time) executive director at Wood's, told me she had a wave of terror shortly before the session began. She had no idea who I was. And she didn't know what the workshop was about—not really—and no knowledge of how it would be delivered. She realized too late, she said, that what she had scheduled could be a disaster!

The workshop conducted that day is vivid in my memory. I remember faces, events, exchanges; certain people and where they were seated; certain exercises and how specific individuals responded. I remember the breaks and what seemed to me to be the flow of the day. And I remember how open, willing, and generous the participants were. Wood's was already something special, already en route to becoming one of the best places in all of Canada to work, but on that day—at least from my point of view—we were figuring it out as we went along.

Since that first workshop, I have had the privilege of returning to Wood's Homes on six, maybe seven, occasions. I have done that same workshop, or variations of it, with the entire Wood's Homes staff; I've done it, as well, with new staff as turnover occurs. Each and every time my experience has been the same: here is an organization comprised of individuals committed to what they are doing.

What a Difference a Leader Makes!
I have worked with organizational leaders from a variety of disciplines. In the process, I have come across a number of superb leaders and have asked myself what these leaders have in common. My answer? They are willing to address difficult issues as soon as they arise, and they expect others in the organization to do the same. They are creative. They solve problems but they also are trying to create something new and better, a vision of some sort. And they have a sense of humour.

They know they are involved in something akin to theatre, and when they have done all they know to do, they move on but not without appreciation for what they learned. Wood's has had one executive director throughout the time that I have had an affiliation with it: Jane Matheson. She is among the very best organizational leaders I have ever known. The above listed characteristics seem to come naturally to her. For over fifteen years, I have been impressed, consistently impressed, with her leadership.

What a Difference a Culture Makes!

Jane is far from alone at Wood's. The many managers and supervisors whom I have come to know seem to me to share a deep commitment to Wood's, or perhaps it would be better to say, to the mission Wood's serves. One person does not a culture make (though a strong leader knows how important a strong culture is to any undertaking). It takes several individuals to create and sustain a healthy, creative culture. And Wood's has always struck me with the overall health of its culture. In my experience, it is a culture anchored to the values of Wood's Homes. Those comprising the culture do not say "no"; they say "yes"—not indiscriminately but with discernment. They do not turn anyone away; rather, they are welcoming.

I suspect that many at Wood's would find these comments surprising. Why would it be otherwise? Sadly, however, it is not always this way. There are organizational cultures that are dominated by fear; cultures that are xenophobic, inward-facing, unwelcoming. Cultures where the centre of gravity holds its own, at best, or declines as the cynicism spreads. I have seen no sign of this at Wood's. I have seen the opposite. And my view is informed by close to twenty eight-hour exchanges with Wood's staff over the course of fifteen years.

I know this is a document to be comprised of stories—one hundred years of stories—as stories make up the lifetime of an organization (or a person). But I think I am telling a story. The story a consultant or trainer tells with respect to an organization where he or she has worked. What is the face of the organization? That is what a trainer sees, the face—the many faces—of the organization. And the face of Wood's is youthful, open, and thoughtful. Of course, there is the occasional exception, but generally speaking, the face of Wood's is one of promise, commitment, and goodwill.

What a Difference a Story Makes!

Stories are important. In a family, the child grows up hearing family stories and from them acquires a sense of what matters and what is possible; so, too, in an organization. New employees are oriented to what matters and to what is possible by the stories told and witnessed. And they then add to the overall story as seems appropriate and possible.

Here's a story that comes to mind as I write this. On the surface, it may not appear to be about Wood's but it is. Some time after 9/11,

I was scheduled to do several days of workshops at Wood's (and maybe one or two other organizations but Wood's primarily). The evening before I was to fly out, I discovered that my passport had expired. No problem, I thought; I had gone through customs in the past with only my driver's license and birth certificate. I then checked and discovered that it no longer was possible to fly into Canada without a current passport. Checking further, I discovered (to my relief) that it was possible still to drive across the border with a valid driver's license plus birth certificate.

I therefore rearranged my flight, looking for the airport in Montana nearest the Canadian border. From there I would rent a car and drive to Calgary. All of the above was full of drama, not some smooth, calm movement from one step to the next. Rather, it was full of: *There's no way this can happen!* And then: *Okay, okay, maybe I can do it this way.*

The next day, I was driving in northern Montana en route to the border. The timing looked fine. I would arrive at Jane's around eight that evening in plenty of time to ready myself for the week. Of course, there is the standard question asked at the border: *Are you here on business or as a tourist?*

I often have been encouraged by Canadians and Americans alike to forego the trouble. *Say you are here visiting friends . . . you're doing that, as well, right? Save yourself the hassle.* I think about it but I always feel uncomfortable about doing that (it's a presentation on ethics, after all). So I always say I am here on business. This question was asked at the border crossing and I gave my answer. As expected, I was invited inside to meet with a customs official.

I have to say that Canadian customs officials are a very impressive bunch. It's all business. There's no messing around, no getting to know one another. And for reasons I should probably examine, I always feel a little guilty when I stand in front of them. It's Sergeant Preston of the Royal Canadian Mounted Police and I'm sure I've been found out.

So, I come as prepared as I know to be: driver's license and birth certificate, yes, but also samples of my training materials along with letters from the organizations where I will be working. Letters indicating that I have been invited, that all in all I'm okay and, in any event, will be leaving the country in a matter of days.

I was called to the counter. The custom's official—my age or younger though he seemed older—examined my material.

"Here's my birth certificate and valid U.S. driver's license," I began. "And here's a letter from Jane Matheson, the executive director of Wood's Homes where I will be working. Maybe you know of Wood's. They have locations throughout the province. You may even know Jane. Do you know Jane?"

"Don't they have anyone else who can teach this?" he interrupted.

"Well, uh, no, not really. I developed the program, and they've been using it for several years. There's no one else who does this training. Do you like basketball?"

"Where are your credentials?"

"My credentials?"

"How do I know you're qualified to teach this?"

"Well, uh . . ."

"Do you have evidence of your training, your university diploma, for example?"

"You want to see my diploma?"

I didn't have it, of course, or any other means of proving to him that I had the training that would be necessary . . . whatever that training would be. So, I said, "Let me see what I can do."

I drove back the thirty miles to the nearest town—I don't remember its name—and stopped in several businesses still open until I found one with a fax machine—it was a pizza shop and bar. I called my wife, told her where she could find the diploma (luckily, I knew), and asked her to take it to FedEx or Kinko's and fax it to me. It took a couple of hours. (The person at the pizza shop didn't realize the fax machine wasn't on.) Eventually, I had a fax copy of my diploma.

I headed back to the border, took a seat, and waited for my customs official to call my name. By now it was 11:30 p.m. I showed him my diploma. He disappeared into a back office for the longest time. I figured he had found spelling errors. Eventually he returned, passed my materials and documentation back to me, and stamped my work permit.

"Welcome to Canada," he said.

We both smiled. "I appreciate the way you guided me through this," I said. "You were very patient and very professional."

He laughed. "Drive safely," he said.

It was midnight. As I went through the door, I looked back and waved. He waved, and we were both smiling.

I drove to Jane's house, arriving (I think) around 2:30 a.m. I found the note that had been left for me, found the downstairs bedroom, and was never so glad to arrive anywhere.

The next day the week of training began as scheduled. Now, I'm not sure I would have gone to this trouble for any other group but Wood's. I like to think I would, but I'm not sure. Wood's has taken my work seriously. It has used it, applied it. I'm extremely grateful. The last thing I wanted to do was not show up for Wood's after Wood's so often had shown up for me.

So, at some point as the above story unfolded, I decided to treat it as a creative exercise. Not immediately. Initially, it was panic: *How stupid! You let your passport expire!* I think it was when I met the customs' official that I became inspired. No matter what, I decided, I would try to create a solution.

This, I believe, is what Wood's itself has done—must have done—in order to have survived one hundred years. I know that a lot goes into the survival of an organization, but the ability to create solutions to problems that arise must be at the heart of it. And not only survive but in the course of time become one of the Top One Hundred Best Workplaces in Canada, and among the Top One Hundred Best Workplaces for Women in Canada. Wood's has been and is an ongoing creative exercise. I know it is so from conversations with Jane concerning problems and obstacles that have arisen and been resolved in recent years. It's inspiring: *To muster the focus and creative energy needed to establish and maintain a standard well above the norm.* It's what every organization aspires to but very few achieve.

It's been an honour for me to be involved with Wood's Homes. Its leadership, its culture (the people who comprise its culture), the story that is Wood's, all has enriched my understanding of what it takes to accomplish something truly distinctive. I'm grateful to be a small part of the story, to have had a bit part, and to have been a witness; and I'm grateful for the opportunity to offer these thoughts on behalf of an organization that I so thoroughly admire.

—David Thomas, PhD

Senior management team at a yearly retreat.

58

Kevin was eleven when I met him. I received a referral from his school saying that he was difficult and his parents needed help, and not much else. Kelly, his mom, seemed relieved that I called and I was coming. We set up a time for me to stop by the following week. I first met the family on a hot day in June.

I got to the house, where Kelly greeted me and invited me into the living room. Kelly was warm and friendly and asked me to wait while she got her three boys, Jason who was fourteen, Kevin, and the youngest, Amos who was nine. They had family pictures on the walls, where all three boys looked happy and healthy. When the boys came into the room I could tell there was something different about Kevin just by the way he walked into the room and sat down.

I introduced myself and talked about my role and asked them some questions about themselves, and then I asked them if I could have some time with just their mother. The boys wanted to go outside and ride bikes around the neighbourhood. Jason and Amos got their shoes on and went out.

The best way to describe Kevin through this fifteen-minute interaction was that he looked as though he wanted to crawl out of his own skin. He was clawing at his clothes and skin, and adjusting himself in his seat when he was seated. He got up to check if the door was locked seven times. He checked to make sure nothing was under the TV stand six times. He asked his mother if he was a bad person thirteen times. He checked to see if the stove was off three times. He asked his mother if he had ever killed anyone two times. He asked if his water was safe to drink and not poisoned five times. In between him asking these questions and getting up to check things, he answered my questions. He said he loved science and math, and he liked being outside with his family hiking and biking.

While his brothers were putting their shoes on, Kevin went to get his helmet, elbow pads, knee pads, wrist guards, his coat, his shoes for biking, socks, and a sweater. He tucked his T-shirt into his pants and his pant legs into his socks. He checked the door again. He had Velcro shoes for biking so shoelaces would not get caught in the bike. He checked under the couch and under the TV. He put his knee guards on over his pants. He asked his mom if he was a good person. He put on his sweater and kept the hood over his head. He checked the door. He put his elbow pads over his sweater. He put his wrist guards on and checked the stove, under the couch, and the door again. He put on his helmet and asked his mom to check to make sure it was on the right way. He asked her to check it again. He asked her if he was going to die. He put on his jacket and zipped it all the way up. It took Kevin thirty minutes to leave the house to join his brothers. When he left I asked Kelly if this was typical. She said it was better than before.

Kevin then burst back into the house and yelled, "I think I killed someone!"

Kelly asked, "What happened?"

He explained that he thought he hit someone with his bike and was sure he had killed someone.

Kelly asked if he had gotten his bike out of the shed yet.

He said, "No."

Kelly asked, "How it could be that you've killed someone with your bike if you don't have it out yet?"

Kevin said, "Right," and instantly seemed to calm down. Kevin was able to go get a book and read by himself while I sat with his mother after that (with a few interruptions).

Kevin had just come home from a long stay at the hospital where he was diagnosed with early-onset schizophrenia. Kevin had a psychologist, psychiatrist, a therapist, occupational therapist, all of whom he met weekly or twice a week. He attended a specialized school program. Kelly had quit her job to make sure he could get the help he needed. Kevin's father, Walter, worked twelve hours a day to support the family and would often put in time on the weekends. When he was off, he took Kevin out to give his wife a break. Amos and Jason helped out as well, by taking him to the park or trying to play games with him.

Kelly said she was exhausted and confused by everything. She went to countless meetings, with countless suggestions, with all of this jargon she did not understand, all of which she needed to make sense of and put into practice for her son. Kelly said most days she was too exhausted to make changes or take action on anything because she was in survival mode and just getting by.

I asked Kelly what kept her going and working so hard for Kevin. Kelly said she kept going for the glimpses of the "old Kevin." The Kevin that was happy and healthy before he got sick. There were times when he was able to ride in the car without constantly checking he seatbelt and asking her to be careful. There were times when he was able to eat on his own without being fearful of being poisoned. There were times when he was just a normal kid. This gave her hope and the ability to give him as normal a childhood as possible. Kelly said that if were up to Kevin, he would be in his room or right next to her all of the time, but the family would not let the mentally ill side of Kevin take over.

Kelly got connected with respite care to give her a break. She got other resources involved so Walter did not have to work so much and could help out. The family made joint plans with all of the professionals involved, so everyone was working toward the same goals with Kevin. The family was actively participating in decisions in his treatment. The family did more activities together where they saw more and more the healthy side of Kevin. The family worked hard at keeping structure and predictability in place for him. Kelly got him connected with a cross-country skier who offered to work with him for free.

Toward the end of my time with Kevin, he went on a mental health retreat with some other students. Over the three days, he participated in a yoga class, did art therapy exercises, played tag, played basketball, ate all of his meals, participated in a drumming circle, slept well, roasted marshmallows, got to the top of a giant swing, and did a ropes course. When it was time to get going each morning, Kevin got his shoes on and went outside. It took him maybe two minutes.

When I think back on Kelly, Walter, Jason, Kevin, and Amos, I think about how easy it would have been to give into the schizo-phrenia diagnosis. I think about how the family took the hard road and how it paid off in the end. When I last saw Kevin he had plans to be a helicopter pilot, he was volunteering in his neighbourhood, and was going to be in a play. Kevin's story is a happy one, which could have been tragic had the family not found the strength to carry on.

59

Summerstock began in the mid-1980s as a summer theatre program that was open to young people who were in care with a variety of social agencies. Eventually, as a result of the kind of enthusiastic response the program got, it became a year-long initiative, featuring a two-month intensive during the summer and culminating in a performance and two short fall and winter experiences. Because it was difficult to offer follow-up across agencies, the theatre program transitioned into an in-house program, solely administered at Wood's.

One summer we decided to set the theatre rehearsals and presentation at Hillhurst. The kids had taken as their theme for the performance the notion of *repair*, of what was needed to repair a home. Repair could mean a lot of things. This theme was explored on several different emotional and prosaic levels, so in addition to working on a script and rehearsing a performance, they also worked alongside staff to actually repair and restore the Hillhurst facility. They painted it. Planted a garden. Dug out a firepit. Repaired a fence. It was intense, hard, physical work—for the staff as well as the kids.

There were challenges. A couple of the kids had issues with solvent abuse; if they were left alone for a fraction of a second they would slip away and find a gas line to cut. Some of the kids had affiliations with gangs. If I wasn't watchful, fights would break out. And, it was what I called, "The Summer of Randys."

There were three Randys in the group that year, and they all had a special knack for generating trouble and getting under my skin. One Randy in particular—Middle-sized Randy—was especially demanding. He slept in most mornings, and staff had to pester him to get out of bed. He was oppositional. Whatever I wanted him to do, he didn't want to do it, or it couldn't be done. He swore. He lied. He got into fights and provoked the other kids. He went on the run for a couple of days. He took every opportunity to tell me that the program sucked, that the script sucked, that drama sucked. He told me I sucked. He exhausted me.

Finally, however, performance day arrived. The group had completed a successful dress rehearsal. Tapers were lit in the garden. The house was fixed up and looked beautiful. A garden had been planted in the backyard, and in addition to vegetables thriving, flowers blossomed. At sunset, a large audience congregated and stood in the backyard to view the performance. The script the kids had developed was very sweet, and their performances were compelling, funny, and honest. Overall, it was great. The kids co-operated, gave everything they had, and as a result the production was witty in places, raw and uncompromising in places, and moving throughout. The group did a great, great job.

After it had finished, snacks were served, and as usual, members of the audience lingered to speak with the cast and compliment them. I was discussing something with someone, I can't remember who, when I felt that prickle you do when you realize someone is watching you. I turned and noticed Middle-sized Randy staring at me. He didn't say anything, just kept looking and I could tell something was up.

"What is it?" I asked.

"I need to talk to you," he hissed, "right now."

"Okay," I replied and waited for him to continue.

"Not here," he said, "in the alley."

"Another problem," I thought, and my heart sank, but said, "All right."

We moved into the alley. The sun had dropped into the far western horizon at this point, and the alley was cloaked in shadow.

"Not here," he said, "farther down."

"Great," I thought. We walked farther down the alley, away from the crowd.

He took a look at me, glanced back at the distant audience to make sure that we couldn't be heard. I was trying to figure out what had gone wrong. In my mind I was testing various hypotheses. Had he stolen something? Had he hurt someone?

"Actually," he said, in a low conspiratorial voice, when he was sure no one was around to overhear, "I kind of like drama."

And once he'd shared that with me, he turned and sprinted back up the alley to rejoin the festivities.

—Clem Martini

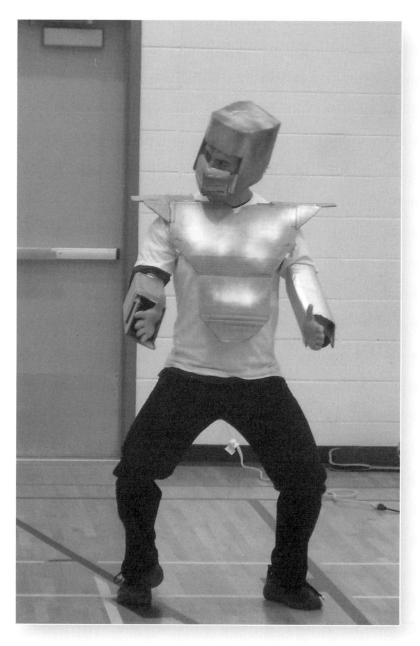

A young person involved in performance at Wood's Homes.

60

At Wood's Homes, a variety of professionals come together to deliver services for young people: counsellors, social workers, therapists, nurses, not to mention the management and support staff. When it comes to core clinical services, however, the most often employed are those with a counselling discipline, trained in two or more years of formal education to work with young people.

However, in my time at Wood's Homes, I have come to realize that these formalities can be crutches that can get in the way of caring for children. Although it is important, counselling training cannot replace the fundamental compassion that comes from wanting to care for and nurture young people who have been mistreated or misunderstood in their lives.

The best example I saw of this was with a co-worker who was employed at the Exceptional Needs Under 12 Program (U12) for two years. She did not come from a background that was counselling-specific; however, her bachelor of fine arts, along with a bevy of life experiences, gave her a unique perspective on young people and on the intense feelings and challenges they often face, especially when living in a residential care facility.

At her core was the belief that milieu treatment was all about nurturing for this unique population, and she did not hesitate to point out to her more scholarly colleagues that a hug and a bedtime story were much more impactful elements of treatment than a lecture on dealing with feelings. She was firmly orientated in a trauma-sensitive context and always conducted herself with the utmost professionalism as it pertained to boundaries and structure. She was, however, always able to find teachable moments in things like baking bread (from scratch mind you, not out of a box), play time (even video games, and she was not afraid to go to bat for the young people on this one), and bedtime.

She attempted—single-handedly—to bring things to the U12 program that had not existed before. She managed an intense sewing schedule, where she would hand-sew beautiful crafts for the children, such as custom curtains for their doors, heavy blankets for their beds (also a useful therapeutic tool), and for each young person graduating from the program, a home-sewn wall hanging.

She engaged the kids in play and craft with an inclusive teaching mentality and took on painting their bathroom windows, which previously did not even have blinds, with stained glass paints, which can still be viewed to this day. Before she left, she also began a project of painting a mural in the Calming Room, so that young people would not feel oppressed by four white walls.

As the little folk went down to bed, she brought in the concept of *dream spray,* which to grumpy adult eyes may have looked like essential oils and water in a spray bottle, but to the children this was an essential part of their sleep safety. They would often invent their own elaborate rituals for bedtime to go along with it.

Long after they went to sleep, she would spend the night cooking and cleaning with diligence and considered it of the utmost importance for young people to eat healthy. She would put all manner of veggies (of the fresh, not out-of-a-bag-in-the-freezer variety) into their food, and encouraged healthy eating wherever possible. Even pizza night was met with homemade dough, which the kids got to make themselves.

I have been with Wood's for a modest ten years and have seen some excellent clinical work happen with young people; however, this individual taught me a valuable lesson that I will never forget: For the young people who come to stay with us, this is their childhood. Sure, they are here to do treatment and that is important, but especially for children under twelve it is the only time in their lives they will be six, or seven, or eight, or nine, or ten, or eleven. Regardless of whether they are in a treatment home or not, this must never be forgotten. Workers should never lose sight of their importance as adults who can nurture, not just lecture, because relationships and moments are what make this agency special.

One hundred years from now, stories like this will be the spark of what will make this agency great, not outcome measures, textbooks, and oblique stats, which are contextual and die when they no longer are relevant.

Nurturing is always relevant, and this individual made a difference in my practice, as well as for those around her because of those messages. Most important, young people are out there in the world today, better people because of what they received while in her care.

—Cameron Kopeck

61

David has a history of accessing EXIT Community Outreach. When his father returns from his truck-driving trips, both David and his mother are physically abused. His mother refuses to do anything about the abuse. EXIT's medical staff verifies this abuse to be true—they can see the results of bruising on his back. EXIT staff have had several conversations with David about Child Welfare getting involved and the possibility of David accessing our Next Steps Program. He is initially worried because his mom will find out and disagree.

David talks with EXIT staff for some time and then says out loud he is really tired of the beatings and is okay with staff calling Child Welfare. He just does not want to leave his mom without support.

David was able to access Child Welfare services and he is currently living in our Next Steps Program. He reports that he is now able to sleep well. He says he now needs help with how to approach his mom about leaving the situation.

62

Editor's Note: The following two stories represent separate parts of an ongoing journey.

62a

Seth has been unemployed for more than two years. He uses the services at EXIT Community Outreach every day. He admits that holding onto a job has been difficult as he often does not show up to work and then gets fired; or he has a pattern of getting paid and just walking away. He has always indicated that he would like to get into the restaurant business but has no experience. EXIT staff tell Seth about the new Culinary Arts Program at Wood's.

Seth spent eight weeks in the program and received his safe food handling certificate as well as the Wood's Homes certificate of completion. In addition he was given a $500 bonus as part of his successful completion of the program. With the support of the staff, Seth secured employment in a local restaurant.

So far, so good!

The 2012 EXIT Community Outreach van.

62b

Dear Staff,

My name is Seth. I'm a former resident of the Wood's Home shelter. It's been four years since my time here and I want to thank you all for being there to support me. With a positive outlook and a real test of adversity, things in my life are turning for the better. I'm a third-year carpenter at SAIT right now and I bartend at night to pay for books and classes. I'm about to start business classes and dream of one day owning my own company.

None of this would be possible without the support your staff gave me. Thank you all, and if you ever doubt, remember you gave me a chance. A miracle. Keep up the outstanding work.

Cheers, I will never forget.

Seth

63

Editor's Note: This story is a short script developed by the young people of the Phoenix Program who participated in a fall theatre session. The title of the play is Chess, *because they had decided to study the game and to think about how it applied to their lives.*

During the creation of this production, the kids first examined the history of the game and then were taught how to play chess—only a couple of them knew initially. They constructed wooden chess boards in their shop classes, sculpted their own chess pieces from clay and fired them in a kiln, played a weekend tournament, and meditated on how the game of chess related to family and their lives. This play— ultimately performed on a giant room-sized chessboard that they had also constructed—was collectively written by the group.

VOICE: Chess.

(*Lights up on kids situated on various squares of an enormous chessboard.*)

ALL VOICES: The chessboard:

VOICE: . . . a board with sixty-four squares of two alternating colours used for playing chess.

ALL VOICES: Chess:

VOICE: A game played by two persons, on a chessboard with thirty-two chessmen.

VOICES: Chess is like war.

VOICE: Chess is like a swordfight.

VOICE: Chess is like the hardest game I ever played.

VOICE: Chess is like life.

ALL VOICES: The game involves

VOICE: Struggle.

VOICE: Strategy.

VOICE: Planning.

VOICE: It takes from the moment you begin playing,

VOICE: To the moment you finish.

VOICE: It takes however long it takes.

VOICE: The object of the game is to

VOICE: Make it to the other side.

VOICE: To succeed.

VOICE: To survive.

ALL VOICES: Chessman:

VOICES: One of several pieces used in playing chess.

VOICE: You are allowed one move per turn.

VOICE: Alternating back and forth.

VOICE: Once you move a chessman, there's no turning back.

VOICE: It can't be put back.

VOICE: It can't be returned to its space.

VOICE: It can't be changed.

VOICE: The King is the most important chessman on the chessboard. Once he is taken, the game is over. In the world I know a King is like my grandpa.

VOICE: He's like the Big Cheese.

VOICE: He's like the most powerful person in my life.

VOICE: He's like me.

VOICE: A Pawn is like a peasant in the Middle Ages. There are lots of Pawns and they have hardly any power. They're the first things that are gotten rid of in the game and nobody much cares about the Pawns when one of them is taken by the other side. In the world I know, a Pawn is like a soldier.

VOICE: It's like a slave.

VOICE: A person I don't like very much.

VOICE: It's like a lot of people I know.

VOICE: It's like me.

VOICE: The Queen is probably the most powerful character on the chessboard. It can move right across the board in one move, and it can move in any direction. Forwards or backwards or diagonally. It's pretty hard to capture the Queen. In the world I know, a Queen is like God maybe.

VOICE: Or like an entire army.

VOICE: Or like my Mom.

VOICE: Moves are difficult to make because once you move a chessman—

VOICE: There's no turning back.

VOICE: It can't be moved somewhere else.

VOICE: It can't be returned to its space.

VOICE: It can't be changed.

VOICE: It's done.

VOICE: Finished.

VOICE: Sometimes you don't want to move.

ALL VOICES: Move.

VOICE: Sometimes you don't know where to move.

ALL VOICES: Move.

VOICE: But you have to—

ALL VOICES: Move.

VOICE: You can't avoid—

VOICE: Moving.

VOICE: You always have to make a decision.

VOICE: There are moves I wish I could take back.

VOICE: But can't.

VOICE: Once you've made your move, it's done.

VOICE: I would take back my disrespect for others.

VOICE: If I could take a move back, I would take back my whole offence cycle. Because it changed everything.

VOICE: I would take back my attitude.

VOICE: I would take back nothing, because everything, the good and bad, have gone in and made up what I am today.

VOICE: There are moves I've made that I've been proud of.

VOICE: The best move I made was listening to a friend talk about his brother dying. I told him how sorry I was and told him that I had also lost a brother who shot himself. It made me feel good to help by listening.

VOICE: The best move I made was choosing to come here. I came with a lot of issues, but I'm leaving and have overcome a lot of those issues.

VOICE: The best move I made was to respect myself.

VOICE: Now I'm making a new move.

VOICE: I have to—

VOICE: Think ahead.

VOICE: I have to—

VOICE: Make a plan.

VOICE: I have to—

VOICE: Move.

VOICE: I have to—

VOICE: Consider my upcoming placement. I'm on probation and that needs to be part of the decision making.

VOICE: My next move will be to get through treatment, and to start trying harder to finish school.

VOICE: I'm going to listen to my peers and staff and stop playing around.

VOICE: I'm going to stop saying "Your mom" about everything.

VOICE: I will try to succeed in my whole life.

VOICE: By starting —

VOICE: And finishing treatment.

VOICE: Move.

VOICE: Now I just have to—

VOICE: Look at the board.

VOICE: Look at my past moves.

VOICE: Make up my mind.

VOICE: Consider my choices.

VOICE: Make up a plan.

VOICE: And move.

64

Karen's father, his two friends, and her brother sexually abused her for over five years. She stood out by her rough nature, strange clothing, and very aggressive and angry behaviour toward anyone who tried to engage with her. She was referred to a Wood's Homes residential program from Manitoba, as she had severed more than fifteen previous placements, most of them foster homes.

She had started to work in the Winnipeg sex trade. She'd beaten another girl almost to death one night and as a result ended up in jail. Following a few months spent serving jail time, she came to Wood's Homes.

Karen's social workers couldn't find organizations to take her, or services that were interested in trying to help her.

She lived at the Bowness Campus for about a year. She ran away a lot during her first four months. She said she did not want to stop working the street. Wood's Homes staff followed her, looked for her on the streets, tried to engage her when she chose to stay in the program, and were continuously searching for that special carrot to draw her into the program and to begin working through her pain. During the first four months she was assaulted twice on the street and once nearly overdosed on drugs.

The staff convinced Karen's mother to come to Calgary to spend two weeks with her and the staff. Her mom was also very worried about her daughter. She agreed to come and, with the support of Child Welfare, flew to Calgary. The program hosted Mom for the entire two weeks. Mom and Karen spent those two weeks involved in intensive therapy, doing fun activities together, and for the first time in years talking about pain and forgiveness.

To everyone's surprise, Karen did not run away even one time during those two weeks. She slept in the same bed with her mom every night. Karen committed herself to finishing treatment, and six months later moved back to Manitoba where she lives with her mom and two younger siblings.

65

My name is Kyle and I live in Ontario. I was a former resident of the Phoenix Program for about two years. I just wanted to let you guys know you changed my life. I know I had serious problems back then and only cared about one person and that was myself.

I had those bad sexual tendencies and you guys sure helped me with changing before I went back in society. I believe group therapy helped me express my feelings after a while cause I remember I was quite shy and not always willing to open up. I am glad I succeeded. Back in society, I never reoffended which I am so happy about.

I remember the staff. I remember Tony, Tracy, Grace—I cannot remember her last name—there was Dale, Joyce. I wish I could thank them personally but I do not think that would be possible. Please get in contact with me. I would appreciate it very much.

PS:

1. Tony was my worker. He did a lot of good for me. I remember I had strong urges to reoffend. He would play these cassette tapes. And that helped.
2. I was looking for ways to contact people. I know we had the journal writing, and the group therapy. I think I was better at journal writing. I wasn't good at talking in front of the group. I was nervous as heck when I first got there. I kind of thought people would be mean, but they were pretty welcoming. I remember Teri, I think.
3. I learned not to reoffend, because I've been on the straight and narrow since. Getting to know different people was great. That was very good.
4. I know I would give up too easily. I got frustrated too quick. I remember running away. A few of us ran away, I don't think we went very far. We just wanted to rebel against the staff. I don't think we were gone too long. But finally I graduated to that Hillhurst place.

66

I came here on a Monday. It was my first time being a program like this. The day was cold and grey and dreary.

I was mad because I never got a chance to say goodbye to a girl I liked at the last facility I was at. I arrived here around noon, and the guys were all roaming around doing their own thing. My first impression was, "They're freaks." But after I said it, I thought about it and realized if they are freaks, then I'm a freak, cause we're all here for the same reasons.

I knew no one here. It was uncomfortable and a little harsh at first. But as time went on, I started to talk and got more comfortable.

67

Editor's Note: These letters were written by several young residents of Wood's Homes, addressed to the then-prime minister of Canada to apprise of him of their situation at Wood's Homes.

Dear Prime Minister,
Here is the thing you don't know about Wood's. It is that the people in the cottages on campus aren't allowed to smoke since you passed a bylaw that minors are not allowed to smoke, so ban the bylaw now!

Dear Prime Minister,
Here is the thing you don't understand about Wood's. If you don't know about us yet, this is a place for adolescent teens who have sexual problems, anger management issues, trust, and more. It is a place for us to learn about skills to manage these feelings, these will help us cope with future issues or problems we may come across, which may set us up for reoffending. I think it would be nice for someone who has the power you have to come and learn a few things from us as well as the staff in this place. I feel that it may be beneficial to us to also learn some things from you, your experiences in dealing with youth over your years of working in politics. Plus, we may look up to you. If you consider this proposal, I would really appreciate it.

Dear Prime Minister,
Here is the thing you don't understand about Wood's. It's too far away from home and I don't like to be that far away. We come here to get treatment and have a better life, but I get sad for my parents.

68

I came to Calgary in 1986 to start the first shelter at the Boys and Girls Club. I had heard a lot about Wood's. One of the things that struck me was the clinical deftness that the organization demonstrated. It also exhibited a real sense of community— like you belonged to something bigger.

When I finally got to Wood's, I became program manager of Phoenix and spent time at the Bowness Campus. I wasn't sure if it was the place for me. I made huge mistakes. I was supposed to manage Habitat, and the program would be open and operated. I didn't ask enough questions, and sometimes I think that is still my problem.

We started getting all these clients from Children's Services. We were working around the clock. I was so angry at the then-director. So when Christmas came, there were no presents. And Jane called and said, "Oh my god, those kids were there and you didn't have presents?" And I had to put a letter on my file. I had to write a letter of discipline. Because I could've asked more questions. I could've asked for help.

The strength of the agency is that it permits you to make mistakes, and learn from them. And then get help from other people. That's the depth of this organization. Had I been somewhere else, I probably would've been fired. But I learned from it, and I'll never do that again.

—Madelyn McDonald

69

Editors Note: The following four entries form a kind of set of stories, a group of writings submitted by young people in programs who attempted to describe what brought them to Wood's Homes, or describe some of the struggles they experienced. I've opted to maintain the spelling and grammar of the original documents, as these, too, are expressions of some of the struggles these young people faced.

...

It started back when I was five years old. When I knew I had to fight back, when I first beated up a bully in grade one. It felt grate to fight, so I continue to fight back and that is why I have my personality in me. I learned how to stick up for myself because I could not depend on eneyone.

...

I have a dvdbitfit [difficult?] groups and hard qusotions so I try to awsswer the qusotion and its hard to awnanswer too so Listen in gropu so I can do my treatment so I can go home and I whet go to treatmet some of the groups are hard so I am doing working hard and I try to think in my mind to say works.

...

When I offended, people thought that I could do better than that. After I got caught, it took me about a month to get past it. How I reacted was like all angry—saying I didn't care. But I felt lonely. I just tried to get past it.

...

When I was growing up, all of my family members weren't very honest with themselves and others. The only time I heard honesty is when someone was drunk. So, honesty is one of my tools to repair my family. It's going to be hard trying to get my family to be honest, but for me it's a very important tool because even as I write this some of my family members can't handle honesty and live in a fantasy world. I don't know how I could make them honest. All I could do is be honest with them, set an example. Once this is accomplished we can be a powerful, communicating family with no secrets or lies.

70

She probably just wanted to make a friend—but the way she went about it and whom she chose as her guide were perhaps not the best. The consequences were dire.

A group of eight adolescents, fifteen years and over, lived together in a Wood's Homes transitional residential program in an area of Calgary that, when then the house was purchased in the 1970s, was a middle-income community—bungalows lined the streets. In fifty years it had become gentrified and this little home (Hillhurst) was quickly looking out of place. Young people who lived there were on their way to independence and were able to live, go to school, and work in a community setting.

It was about three days before Christmas. She had younger visitor. The young man who befriended her this particular evening was aggravated by one of his housemates and talked her into lighting a fire under his pillow. He wanted the housemate to know he was aggravated and that he had power over him . . . that kind of thing (even though he got someone else to do it for him).

The fire caught quickly. The staff were terrific, so everyone safely left the house without too much panic. The fire department came quickly, too. The house was not burnt to the ground, but it was rendered uninhabitable. The Christmas presents were destroyed. We were definitely on the neighbours' radar screen now! Luckily, there were other living arrangements for the kids.

The staff spent quite some time trying to figure out who set the fire. This is not unusual with troubled kids—waiting and mining for the truth. The staff suspected others and were both surprised and shocked when she tearfully confessed. Her? No way, they said. The police were called. She was charged with arson.

Her social worker called and said she had already purchased a plane ticket for her to return to her home community as of course we would not want her around. The staff said: "What? There is no way she is escaping the consequences of this and of course we will not give up on her."

So, she stayed and went to jail for some time. When she was being released, she appeared before the judge, and he asked her if there was something she wanted to say.

She said, "I cannot believe they forgave me."

The William Taylor Learning Centre, Parkdale Campus.

He said, "I cannot believe it either."

I do not know where that girl is now or how well or poorly she may be doing, but I do know that forgiveness has a powerful effect on people who make mistakes.

And—who among us doesn't find him or herself in that category?

As an aside . . . we decided to sell that house and land rather than rebuild. I wrote a letter to every neighbour on that short street. The letter thanked them for their patience with us over the past years and for including us in the community. I received one response. That letter said we had taught their family many things and opened their children's eyes to other worlds and the challenges others faced. They said they would miss us. And it just takes one response like this to make it all worthwhile.

71

Editor's Note: This story resulted from an interview with three individuals who were intimately involved in restructuring the pedagogy and delivery of educational outcomes at Wood's Homes: Carolyn Barker, Jeannie Everett, and Janet McFarlane.

CAROLYN: What we worked on together was an entire redesign of our school program. The partnership between Wood's and the Calgary Board of Education, because of what we said we wanted to do, wasn't functional—so we blew up the school. Both figuratively and really. We totally, *physically* renovated the schools and we completely *rethought* how school should operate. And we completely changed the partnership. And by "we," I mean the organization.

JANET: That would have been 2001, right? Because I had just come back from maternity leave.

CAROLYN: I can probably speak to what the experience was like prior to that. As a result of never saying no, we were stretched very thin, because we had all these kids with very high needs, and very limited resources. So part of "the blowing things up" was truly focusing on these kids.

JEANNIE: And finding other services and other ways to support them—because we just couldn't be all things to all kids. But if we looked to our satellite programs for support, for instance, there were solutions to be found. This isn't the only place. This was about inclusive approach to education; it wasn't all or nothing. And we couldn't carry on the way we had been . . . we had our hands full.

CAROLYN: Back in 1996, in preparation for "blowing up of the school," Jane got involved in the Capital Campaign. Jane and I have memories of going to lunch with these prospective donors, trying to raise funds for the school— my job was simply to tell interesting stories about the kids. And we would try to persuade them to donate. And they did.

JANET: I can remember when you came with David to look at the school. Do you remember that first graduation? It was just . . . chaos.

JEANNIE: It was crazy. Kids were all over the place. Nobody was listening.

CAROLYN: That was the moment. That was the moment when we realized it couldn't get worse than this. It wasn't respectful. It wasn't productive. It felt like anything we did would be better.

So then . . . we rolled up our sleeves and started the work. And we started to develop business plans. And we created curriculums.

JANET: But even before we did that, we had a pizza party with the kids in the new school—because Jane was adamant that the kids should be the first ones in.

CAROLYN: Before that, the focus had been on trying to contain kids who were having trouble in the system. And all the normal things related to their education—things that kids generally do in school—were lost.

JEANNIE: That's good phrasing. Containment. Just getting them there and keeping them there.

CAROLYN: And some of the "keeping them there" was bogus. Remember, there was that classroom where they just showed *Beavis and Butthead* all day long?

(*General sounds of disgust.*)

JEANNIE: It was an evolution from containment to attainment. That was the transition. We began doing literacy tests.

JANET: We started the Duke of Edinburgh awards.

CAROLYN: We started a Scout group. The Phoenix kids loved it.

JANET: For the kids who weren't really that focused on academics, we started a work program.

    Then there was the relationship we developed with Theatre Calgary, and they gave us tickets, and we started to take kids to the theatre.

    The first show we brought the kids to—I think it was *Anne Frank*—was so great. We did some prep work with them. And then after the show, the kids got to do a backstage tour. The artistic director, Ian Prinsloo, was very passionate about helping the kids.

JEANNIE: We started a basketball team. We were playing against the other smaller schools. I remember we bought some black basketballs, didn't know they would leave marks on the gym floor.

JANET: I remember looking at the off-campus portion, and bringing them for golf lessons, and COP [Canada Olympic Park], and I tried to get one student into fencing, climbing, get them into the community, giving them experiences.

CAROLYN: The other thing that we did with that school was to ensure that if anything got broken or vandalized, it got fixed immediately.

JEANNIE: We focused on literacy scores. I remember seeing the literacy scores rising, and getting excited.

CAROLYN: We went through accreditation—do you remember?

JANET: Oh God, yes.

CAROLYN: It was accreditation where you had to describe the processes you went through to achieve goals. We had to think through why we did what we did. We had to be clear.

JEANNIE: I think, when we started to formally measure kids' achievements, that's when we got going. And we had a bit of a task to convince people that these kids could actually achieve. We had to convince people outside of the organization, yes, but we had to convince people *within* the organization, too. Convince them that regardless of the fact that this kid has blown out of your class once a day, that he was still capable of achieving. There was that validation. The sense that these kids could be who we thought they could be.

JANET: We worked with the cottages. Talking with the people there and making them see themselves as the parents. Making the school staff and the cottage staff work together. Making school staff understand that you cannot just kick the kids out and have them go back to the cottage. And making the cottages understand you have to get the kids to school. If school starts at 9:00, it's your job to make sure the kids are there.

JEANNIE: That was a memorable time.

CAROLYN: This transition was happening . . . it was really happening. We got three good years—from 2001 on. The planning happened prior to that, for sure, and it was the planning that made it happen. But then once it got going, it hit a kind of rhythm—and suddenly it found its way.

Looking back, you see the foundations, but you can also see the evolution. I can see the whole evolution. I think back to that time now, and it's unbelievable. It was no longer a containment. It wasn't a drop-in anymore.

JEANNIE: I went in there twice lately and you wouldn't have believed it. The kids were quiet, respectful, focused. I don't mean to brag, but there was something special happening there.

72

Two years ago I was one of many young people living on the streets. At the age of fourteen, I ran away from home and turned to a life of prostitution. I battled with myself daily over the kind of life I was living, and the kind of life I wanted to be living. It was impossible for me to look at myself in the mirror, while dressed in stiletto heels and clothes that would give my parents a heart attack, and say to myself, "I'm a good person. I like who I am."

It took me seven years of self-victimization and trauma on the streets before I realized that it wouldn't get any better until I made a commitment to myself to change my lifestyle. This meant I had to move from my home and disassociate myself from the people and places I was frequenting. Several months later I was given an opportunity to prove to myself and society that I could follow through with that commitment. And now, fourteen months later, I am a youth and family counsellor aide. I was given an opportunity to take part in a program called Passages.

Passages was a program, in partnership with Canada Employment Immigration, Mount Royal University, and Wood's Homes, that guided young people with a past street life experience who desired to make a better life for themselves. Passages gave me the opportunity to learn about myself and explore alternatives to the lifestyle I used to live. It was like they provided me with a vehicle and a map with many different avenues to explore. I chose the roads I wanted to take and drove myself there. I have finally found the contentment in my life that was missing. But it wasn't easy. It was an uphill battle all the way, and I struggled with many issues that I thought I had left behind. Passages gave me the support and guidance I needed to continue surviving and achieving. I worked hard to get to this point and I am proud of myself. But my journey is far from finished.

I now have a new set of goals to accomplish. My career goal is in social work, and there are many steps I need to take to complete that goal. It will be a lot of hard work with many new challenges. But it's worth it and so am I.

73

Well, prior to living at Wood's, I lived at another institution called Michener Services, once called the Michener Centre. I lived there through desperation, through misdiagnosis. I was very grateful to be finally placed at Wood's. When I got to Wood's I was as happy as anything.

I'd had some very bad experiences at Michener and had a very bad experience with one of the boys who lived at Wood's, too. He used to bully me, and pick on me a lot, and one female staff who was only on night shift on weekends, she was very, very rude to me. She told me with her mouth that she liked me, but her attitude was very grouchy. And this young fellow who worked on regular shifts, was the type of person who pushed people around. And that still haunts me. That boy still haunts me.

Since I left Wood's thirty years ago, this is the first time I have told anyone these stories. Most of the staff at Wood's were very, very nice. All the teachers who worked there were very nice. I guess one of the best experiences was with one of the girls who lived in the same house as me. She told me that she loved me and treated me sweetly. And she thought I was one of the best kids in her eyes. She was an All-or-Nothing person. I had every respect for that person. On the other hand she had a very, very, very bad temper when she got upset, that's what I mean when I say she was an All-or-Nothing person.

Peter was one of the individuals who worked in the place where I was. He was a terribly Hot-and-Cool person. I mean he was hot in terms of being very good, and cool in terms of being a cool person. I believe Peter was my favourite male worker. He remembers me fondly, vividly, and well. Believe it or not, I have every respect for him. It's a little hard to explain why. He was a very strict disciplinarian. He took no guff from anyone. So hard-core was he that this one girl that was there—when I saw Peter for the first time in almost nine years—Peter told me that she said she thought he behaved like a dictator might behave in Germany. But I remember when I saw people misbehaving around him it made me feel very ashamed.

I remember him saying to me this time, "I only say things once around here." I sort of agree that Peter was very strict, but he was also jocular; he liked joking around, he was pleasant and polite in the way he behaved, and he stuck out as a pleasant person, he was just a very good person to be around. I can tell you something that he said to me, like I was asking if he had heard what had happened in the house the other day, he said to me, "Michael, I'm always aware of what goes on in this house, nothing is news to me," and that made me respect him even more.

I think more of the good things about him than the bad things. He is one person I would want to see again.

—Michael

74

I didn't know what was going on. I thought my home life was normal—that everyone went through that. No one believed me when I told them about what my mom and stepdad were doing to me. I didn't feel like a priority at home, and I ran away a lot.

When I arrived, I remember Bernie being at the door. I very vividly remember we were sitting, me on the fireplace ledge and Bernie on the couch across from me. It was, or seemed to be, just the beginning of winter—the fireplace was on and Christmas was approaching.

What really astounded me was that I could just be myself. Bernie was the first person that told me I was okay. He made me feel like a person.

75

I was mistreated by my stepmother and uncle. My job was always to do the housework and cook, and take care of all the children before and after school. I wasn't permitted to leave the house and had to keep up my duties even if I didn't feel well. I was forced to sleep on the floor. I was very stressed.

But I went to school every day and I remember how much I loved Mondays because that was the day I could leave the house and be free for a while.

Eventually I came to know and trust a school counsellor and told her a little bit about what was happening at home. Somehow word leaked out that I had shared my story so my uncle beat me very badly. He threatened me if I told anyone again.

So I was very afraid. But during the school summer break,

I kept in touch with my guidance counsellor. I had her phone number. She was very worried about me and eventually phoned Children's Services.

Sometimes when I am alone, I think about how much Wood's Homes has given me. I hope you all know how much they have changed my life. I have a new family and they live at Wood's Homes.

76

Raymond came to Wood's Homes U12 Program (for youth, ages six to twelve who have experienced trauma and maltreatment) at the age of seven. He came from a foster home—the third one because he was unable to manage his temper tantrums and violent behaviour.

When Raymond arrived at the program, we found he had an extensive family history of involvement with prostitution, poverty, exposure to adult sexual material, and Child Welfare. He'd also been exposed to cocaine prenatally, which impacted him cognitively and developmentally. Raymond was conceived as the result of a prostitution relationship that had evolved over time. He didn't know his birth date.

Raymond stayed at U12 for a year. Within that time he became a permanent ward, was reconnected with his parents to say good-bye, and during this process found out his real birth date! Raymond used art therapy extensively to uncover his trauma history and made considerable progress in managing a structured routine and home environment.

Raymond eventually transitioned into a foster home specifically equipped to help him with his mental health and developmental disabilities. Raymond has been there for four years and started grade six this fall.

77

One of my most incredible experiences was an opportunity that came through Wood's Homes. In July 2011, I had the honour of accompanying a former Wood's Homes client from Lethbridge, along with Madelyn McDonald and a Fort McMurray client, to meet Prince William and the Duchess of Cambridge, Kate Middleton.

Graphic emblem for the U12 Exceptional Needs Program.

Adding to the excitement was the secrecy leading up to the event at Calgary Zoo due to security measures for the royal couple. We pored over the invitation wondering what "royal etiquette" meant, and exactly how formal "business attire" is when you are meeting the future King of England. We practised and critiqued curtsies and hoped they would shake our hands before we actually had to try to execute a curtsy.

When the big day finally arrived we headed to Calgary in our finest new clothing and, between moments of giggly disbelief, my young companion wondered over her good fortune being chosen for this experience. We met up with our equally lucky counterparts and headed to the event. There was no small amount of pride and, yes, smugness at being able to walk past the eager crowd of royal watchers and media, flash our fancy invitations, and be granted entrance! We could hear the moment the royal couple arrived by the increase in volume from the crowd. After quick hair, makeup, and curtsy checks (again), we were ready. Our hearts quickened as the moment was upon us, and it couldn't have been more perfect—well, maybe if they'd let us bring our cameras for a picture of us smiling with Prince William and Kate.

They were a lovely couple. They asked all the right questions, were sincere in hearing the girls' stories, and dazzled us with their graciousness and respect. By the end of the day, I think it's safe to say we were all floating on cloud nine. It was an amazing, unforgettable experience, and it was made all the more special being able to witness two of our young clients tell their stories of struggle and success and have them truly heard by royalty.

—Kimberly Wasylowich

78

I'm thinking of a Ghost River trip we took. It was a six- or-seven-day trip. We took a van and were dropped off. The location was very remote. We drove up along an old dry river bed—the van could barely get in—and I remember thinking, "This isn't going to be an easy little camping trip." We were hiking six to seven hours each and every day. A couple of the hikes involved big climbs and, although we started off with excited, motivated kids on day one, two or three days later it was a different thing entirely. We had seven kids. I can remember those kids so vividly.

Every day we would hike: fording rivers, crossing brush, climbing up and over the Aylmer Pass with kids between twelve and seventeen. This was back when kids smoked a little more frequently than they do now, so they had to work. We'd tell them you don't want to eat around bears, but we'd find trail mix dropping out of their sleeping bags. These were tough kids, they'd seen a lot. When we would say we were on our own, that didn't faze them.

The part that stands out for me the most was that there was this young man, the most notorious kid in my tenure, he used to get this psychosomatic neck pain. I really didn't get it—there were nights when he'd be crying, and it was all connected to his trauma. So, he'd had a night of this neck pain, and he wouldn't get up to go hiking the next day. I was designated to stay back. They didn't want me to stay where he could see me, they wanted to let him work it out, but I was to stay behind and keep a look out. He cried for a few more hours, then he stood up, and that's when I jumped up and pretended to be walking back. It made me appreciate what some of these kids have gone through. That a kid would lie there, his head on a rock, crying for all that time, feeling all that . . . pain. It made me realize what the histories of these kids were like.

After that, he was okay. I was just surprised by the significance of that—for me. At one time, I wondered if it was attention-seeking behaviour, but for all intents and purposes he was alone—he never looked up to see if I was there. I understood then how real that pain was for him. It wasn't him trying to play it up. That was my first year.

Those early outdoor experiences were so important. I wish we had the same ability to organize those today. Because I think for those kids the traditional kinds of therapy don't really work. But when you get into the backcountry, it amplifies everything. Everyone becomes vulnerable. This wasn't some trip camping along the road. We were out there.

—Ryan Clements

79

Aala is a grade-eight student at Wood's Homes' William Taylor school. She has refugee status and a traumatic family history. She is unsure of the identity and location of many of her family members. She currently lives in group care in the community. Aala is verbally and physically abusive to staff and peers, and there are concerns about her promiscuity in the community. Aala was placed in the all-girls classroom at William Taylor Learning Centre.

I worked with Aala every school day, as I was the support worker for her classroom. She developed a positive bond with classroom staff and used many of the resources available to her, including art resources in the "chill space" in the classroom. Aala's engagement with the school was slow but consistent. She is now back in grade nine at William Taylor and even sang at a recent learning celebration there. Her love of music is fostered and encouraged every day.

80

Artur's parents called the Community Resource Team (CRT) stating that Artur spends seven to eight hours a day playing violent video games. While he does attend school, they are concerned that he does not do anything else. The video game playing causes contention in the home; they argue about this daily. On one occasion, Artur's father hit him as they fought about his computer use, and the police were called. Artur's father had a difficult time understanding this as in Russia using corporal punishment is not illegal. The police suggested they seek some community supports, such as counselling.

CRT staff met with the family. There was a great deal of anger and disagreement as Artur argued with his parents. It was suggested that the family do an experiment—allowing Artur to earn video game time. This was written down in a contract. The parents were also encouraged to lessen some expectations of their son, such as achieving higher grades (Artur was achieving high eighties) and demanding that he go swimming every day. It seemed that these things were culturally motivated, but Artur was pushing against this as he adapted to this new culture in Canada.

81

Abbas left home at the age of fourteen when a local gang recruited him. He says he has been shot at four times and was in a violent altercation where he required forty stitches to close the wound. He is currently at the Calgary Young Offender Centre where he met with our staff who spoke with him about our Culinary Arts Program. He is interested and staff have made the referral. He says he is ready to leave gang life and this would be a great opportunity for him.

Postscript
Abbas did not show up to the program. Staff were informed by a friend of his that he was found murdered in a local park. The friend believes that it was gang related, but no one is talking about what they think happened.

82

My involvement with Wood's goes back to 2000 or a few years before, helping them with the process of strategic planning. We've done that together maybe three or four cycles. So together we've developed a strategic plan, and an action plan.

These stories are related to the process of getting there. And perhaps the commentary on how they did this—and how they did this differently and how they did it well.

Wood's Homes is a big believer in planning and having participants engage in the process. What Jane (the CEO) does initially is draw together a team—and these are big teams, sometimes sixty people. This is enormously useful for getting a sense of the broader world.

I describe this process as a funnel. You start off with all these people and questions. What do you see on the horizon? What are the other agencies doing? What are the needs of the clientele? Then we narrow the focus as we look to where Wood's is heading and decide on the priorities over the next five years. Wood's is good at engaging this broad group initially. Jane will gather individuals from across the organization—front line, admin, board members—and they are tasked with things to do, broken into sub-teams, and asked to consult with external stakeholders. Some will talk to neighbours in the area.

Wall poster created during an annual retreat.

Some will consult with clientele. Some will communicate with other agencies. So you gather a lot of information about the organization. This information is invaluable as you plan for the future.

I always hold up Wood's as an example to other organizations, because Wood's is totally fearless. It's their hallmark. They open their arms and are very inclusive.

The participants are always very enthusiastic. Say thirty people show up. It's planning, after all. Nobody likes to do this stuff. But they show up enthusiastically. Another hallmark. And not only do they go through this plan, they are very good at *living* it. They translate the literature into their work plan and brochures.

And on the fearlessness issue, you have to remember that you're asking a bunch of questions of people who are going to be fundamental drivers of where the organization is going. Many organizations are very cautious about what they ask of frontline staff or people outside of the organization. You end up asking the funders pretty blunt questions: What do you think about Wood's? What do you like about them? What don't you like about them?

You have to have a pretty good degree of confidence to pose these kinds of questions to your funders. Interestingly enough, they always get good response.

—John Galloway

83

Elsie came to the Stabilization Program from Manitoba for an assessment. She came because of her involvement in gangs and her drug use. In fact, the entire family was involved in gangs and drugs. Elsie was born with missing digits on her left hand due to her mother's substance abuse while pregnant. She wouldn't show her hand, or talk about it.

She often showed serious attitude but could be endearing and humorous. While at Stabilization, Elsie opened up and connected well. She transitioned into the Catalyst Program as she was deemed to be in need of more intensive treatment.

She then had some difficulties focusing on her treatment and fell back into some of her previous difficulties. She is currently awaiting sentencing for one of her previous crimes.

84

I could hear them flipping through the papers one by one and people whispering about the content to each other around the table. At this point I thought it would be better to not look up yet. My palms started to sweat, and I didn't know what my future was going to be.

I was prepared for the worst. I thought to myself, I haven't been this nervous since going to the principal's office in grade school.

It was a fall day when I received a phone call on my day off from my team leader at Wood's Homes. I was requested to meet with a committee resulting from several incident reports that I was involved in. My team leader told me that this wasn't a good thing and that the acting CEO, another Wood's Homes director, and our clinical consultant would be there to review them with us. He told me to prepare for the worst, as it didn't look good since I was involved in all of these restraints and in fact took the lead, or so it seemed to read in the reports.

I asked if I would be fired, as we had a no restraints philosophy and I did about ten restraints in a rotation work period. He said, "Well, we'll see. Maybe you will be put back on probation. The person filling in for J. M. can be very tough and there's not very much understanding when it comes to this stuff. Just be prepared for the worst, don't say much, and just answer the questions."

I was at Parkdale for 1:00 p.m. and started walking up to the Admin Building and down to the meeting room. Everyone was already there. I opened the door and headed in.

When I lifted my head, there was complete silence. I quickly read over the incident reports during that time, and though there were things I could have done differently, in the moment of the incidents, I didn't.

The acting CEO looked at me and said, "You must have had a few really tough work rotations."

I didn't know how to respond, or if this was a rhetorical question. I also just assumed she would start getting mad at me and tell me I sucked at my job. The others around that table also agreed with her. This wasn't what I was told and/or expected. I expected a really mean woman who would tell people how to do their job and let them know if they weren't doing it right.

For the next few hours we discussed everything around ideas that I had and what they felt I could try next time, remembering that we have a no restraint philosophy. As I was about to leave the room, she turned to me and said, "You have potential. Lead with your heart and you will be great."

From that day forward, as a young staff, I took a few things with me from that meeting: I realized that you can only listen to one-third of someone else's perspective on an individual and their experiences. Also, I realized I was there to learn and grow—it was okay to make mistakes.

85

It's not often I get asked the question, "You've worked at Wood's Homes a long time, why do you stay?" I believe the person asking is asking for two reasons:

1. He is carrying a letter of resignation in a back pocket and needs inspiration to stay.
2. She needs a boost or a pick-me-up because she has likely had the day, week, or month from outer space, and just needs a reminder that she is not crazy to come back to her work tomorrow.

When I go to answer this question, I am like an episode from a sitcom: my eyes become foggy, and then, with a harp playing in the background, we fade into experiences I have had over the years. What I keep coming back to is that every time something out of the norm happened to me, I always had a manager who had my back.

Let me be clear on what I mean by "had my back." Sometimes we forget having someone's back doesn't mean 100 per cent supporting her in her choices, but being truly honest, as ugly as it gets, and then being patient to help her work through it. That is something I have always been able to expect from my supervisors here at Wood's. Although there were a few occasions when I didn't realize until after that my supervisor was actually looking after my best interests. Painful learning lessons don't always go noticed in the moment. But I could always count on that supervisor to be around when I did come to my senses and realize, "Okay, you were being tough because you cared about me," and "You cared because you wanted me to understand the parallel processes between myself and my work with my staff, and clients."

In starting my journey to become a manager, I wanted to know how I would know I had impact on my staff, like my leaders had on me. The funny thing is you find out in the least of expected circumstances.

I remember walking out the door of a program I ran (and by "ran," I mean I was a brand-spanking-new team leader). My experience prior had been working frontline in this program for a couple of years. I felt moderately content that I had accomplished a few things on my must-do list.

I tried not to obsess over this to-do list. I thought to myself, "What really matters at the end of the day? My kids are getting quality care—check. My staff are starting to come around and we are developing as a team—check."

As I got into my car and drove off for the rest of the evening, I remember having a feeling in the pit of my stomach. "It wasn't there when I woke up this morning," I thought. "What could this feeling possibly be?" As I was driving home, I tried to convince myself that I had done my best, and blah blah blah—all that positive self-talk we get in a habit of giving ourselves when we are trying to convince ourselves of something.

When I got home, I couldn't shake the feeling. I tried to ignore it like the drunk uncle at a holiday gathering who has had too much to drink, but no one cares to tell him. So, I got lost in whatever it is you try to do to stay busy after a day of working with some tough kids.

Just as I was getting ready for bed, my work phone rang. I answered it without hesitating—it is bedtime, the toughest time of the day for our youth, which means the toughest time of day for our staff. It was one of my staff who had been working the day shift. I looked at the time and thought, "Oh, Jamie, is working overtime, and now she is calling for me to okay her staying late—I bet it's her paperwork for the day that she struggles to get in on time."

She says, "Hey Kiran."

"Hey Jamie, what's up?" I ask. There's a dead silence on the other end. "Hello? Jamie? Can you hear me?"

I hear crying on the other end, so I ask what's going on. She tells me that when she got home a few minutes ago, she found her aunt, who she was living with, in her room, dying. I tried to choose my words carefully, to respond without panic. I remember asking her to repeat what she had just said. In that moment, I remember having this terrible feeling of being overwhelmed. I thought, this isn't a crisis about my kids in my program, this is not work related—what am I supposed to do? A kid on the roof of a building, I can help with that; a parent telling us she is not picking her child up at the end of the five-day stay, sure no problem, I got that one down; even a youth cutting his wrists and smearing the blood on the glass windows to prove a point—no problem, I can help (and yes, for the record all three of these things happened in my first six months as a team leader).

Then it dawned on me—this staff had no family out here, she was from another province, had only moved here less than a year ago, and her only family was her aunt. Through her sobs, she began to explain her aunt had overdosed on pills. She had called 911. The paramedics were on their way, but the reason for calling me was to plan for her day shift tomorrow morning.

As a new team leader, I quickly learned that I played a bigger role to the staff than I thought. Yes, she called me to plan for her shift tomorrow, but she was really calling me for comfort. We spent countless hours a day together; we sat through supervision, where we discussed some vulnerable things . . . not only was I watching my staff group, but more important *they* were watching *me*. They were paying attention to what I said, how I said it, and so on. I served a role outside of being her boss. How did I know this? Because, as soon as I hung up, I called *my* boss. I didn't go to my husband, or call a friend. Instead, I called my boss, because he had been there for years and he would understand that (a) crazy things happen outside of our programs, and (b) we do something, anything, to help.

I remember when he answered I burst into tears. I explained the pressure I felt because being a manager meant more than just managing between the hours of 9:00 to 5:00. He actually chuckled a little, because he got that I'd had my "aha moment." All along I was waiting for this big life-saving thing to occur in my program, where my staff would respond with things like, "Wow, she really is wonder woman, she really is the greatest supervisor." When all along, it was the little things I was doing in between that led Jamie to believe she could count on me to help her in the moment of a crisis—her crisis.

So, when people ask me why I choose to stay here, I tell them: Because it feels right. Because I like being part of something extraordinary.

—Kiran

86

Beth became involved with the Forest Lawn Program and Children's Services the day after her daughter was born addicted to cocaine. Beth's life had been filled with intense daily drug and alcohol use and domestic violence with her partner. She struggled to stay clean, but even after attending treatment for several months she continued to make choices that did not put her daughter first.

Beth has been working with Wood's Homes Family Support Network for the last thirteen months and has attended all organized visits with her daughter over the past seven months. Beth has also attended addiction treatment twice, completed domestic violence programming, and is currently disengaged from her daughter's father. She now has sleepovers with her daughter on a weekly basis.

87

Rita grew up in an affluent family. Her parents were at their wit's end. They tried counselling but Rita's behaviour continued to be out of control. She slammed doors, broke things, hit her sisters, was gone for days at a time, and missed a lot of school. She was hospitalized for an overdose of ecstasy. Her parents researched residential programs and found Wood's Homes Exceptional Needs Program. Rita lived in the program during the week and went home on weekends.

After the first month in treatment, Rita disclosed that a family "friend" had sexually abused her. Through intense counselling and with the support of her parents, Rita was able to begin to heal.

She tells us that she has had some rocky times—she's wary of people, doesn't trust easily, and continues to struggle with self-esteem. But she recently graduated from SAIT, has a good job, and gets along great with her family. She said Wood's Homes allowed her to "make changes that led her into the light, rather than staying in the darkness."

88

Marco experienced significant violence in the home as a young child. In the end, the police removed his father. Then Marco had an accident while playing that led to a phobia of eating. He had been fed intravenously for the past three years by the time he arrived at the Exceptional Needs Program. The family lives in significant poverty and Mom struggles to keep things in order for Marco and his two siblings.

Marco participated in summer programming at the Exceptional Needs Program and was encouraged to take risks and try new things. As a result of this, through the activities he participated in, he attempted to eat. By the time of his discharge from the program he was eating solid food, and his medical team was confident that they could remove his intravenous tube shortly. He also started to attend school regularly, and continues to do so.

89

A young lady around seventeen years old stands quietly at the door, looking longingly into the shelter. The staff stands to respond to her presence and she is gone as quickly as she arrived. Moments later she appears again and a repeat of the past performance occurs. This time the staff unlocks the door and then heads back to the desk.

Within minutes the girl is at the door, this time no physical response from the staff and the young lady pulls at the door. We think she is surprised when it opens but committed at the same time to enter. She comes in and asks the purpose of the shelter, and if she can use the shelter.

A complete intake is done, the regular questions asked. Who are you? Where are you from? How can we be of service? The usual myriad of questions that are required to gain a good understanding of who these kids are and what their immediate needs might be.

Darlene does not seem to be any more needy than any of the other youth who have used the shelter, yet there is something about her that can't be nailed down.

As staff probe to try and get a handle on her, she begins to appear agitated and starts to talk as though she does not need the services.

The staff press on as some of the information is required before a client can utilize the services. Darlene understands and allows a basic question and answer format to occur. Once this process is completed, Darlene is assigned a bed and a locker. She puts some things on the bed, and to everyone's surprise she walks straight to the door and leaves.

Two or three days pass before we hear from her again. One evening she shows up and apologizes for her behaviour and asks if she can come in. We are here to help and not judge so she is allowed in. She eats a good meal, changes her clothes, and off she goes again.

What was going on? Why is this girl doing this? We only want to help her and provide a safe place for her to be. It was decided that she must not have understood the expectations of the shelter and that we would present them to her if she returned.

Well, she did return and, yes, we went over the expectations with her and had her repeat them back to us, which she did quite well. This process went well, we thought. We prepared her a meal; she ate, showered, and went to bed. Within minutes she was walking by the staff, and you guessed it—Darlene has left the building!

Time went on, other youth moved in and out and Darlene continued her routine. Every few days popping in, giving us just enough to bite the hook, and BOOM she would be gone. Darlene abused this privilege a few more times, coming later and later each time.

Finally she was told that if she did not stay the next time she came in, she could not stay at all. We're not a changing room; we are a youth shelter. If she wanted to meet our expectations, she would be welcome.

As it turns out, the very next time she came she did stay—but what a sad, sorry situation it was. She had been beaten by her boyfriend. Darlene told staff that she was sleeping and awoke to him hitting her around the face, leaving two black eyes. She never spoke about that incident after that.

Darlene stayed on for a couple of days and in that time, staff was able to learn that she had been using crack cocaine on a regular basis and prostituting to pay for the habit. These things would explain her using the shelter on a temporary basis, as she had.

—From the Lethbridge Shelter's collection of stories and poems, *Worn Soles, Lost Souls*

90

I started working for Wood's Homes almost two years ago and would constantly hear people talking about the *Wood's Way*. This term was used in so many different contexts. ("We run team meetings like this because it's the Wood's Way." "We work with children and their families using the Wood's Way.") that I began wondering if those people really knew what the Wood's Way was.

Over the past two years, I've come to learn that there isn't just one Wood's Way; it's more of a global concept as opposed to a hard and fast rule. Some Wood's Ways made instant sense; others took a while to make sense. I'll share with you some stories of my first few managers' meetings and the Wood's Way.

I was hired in a bit of an unconventional manner. Not only did I need a work visa, but I was also five months pregnant at the time of hiring. How I got hired is a whole other story but, to make a long story short, my first managers' meeting I had to (a) introduce myself and (b) inform thirty strangers that I was pregnant and that I would be taking a quick maternity leave (three months) and then return. Talk about awkward.

In my head I was thinking, "I get having to tell the people immediately impacted by this, but why do I have to tell everyone now?? This doesn't even affect them!" Maybe a little context would help you understand my rationale. My previous employer was a state government back in the United States, and they operated completely differently. There wasn't any conversation about group process; it was more of an every man for himself atmosphere, and I don't mean that as negatively as it sounds. It was just the culture, and people were used to having to do more because there would come a time when they would need someone to do it for them.

Pregnancy, for example. You did your job, no matter how difficult, until you went into labour. Then you were done for the eight to twelve weeks you took off, and then you were back to work. People didn't even empty their desks. As a manager, your staff would either report to someone else for those weeks, or were left to wander blindly. Fingers crossed.

So that was my awkward first managers' meeting. I was figuring that the second one would be a lot less awkward. No such luck, as it turned out, but at least this time I wasn't in the proverbial hot seat. This time, this seemingly nice HR lady stands up and reminds the group to please fill out any HR-related forms correctly as they've still been getting a lot of errors despite telling people how to fill out the forms and then attempts to sit back down. Our CEO, Jane, stops her and asks her to clarify who. In an attempt to be polite, the HR manager says, "Oh, you know, it's an issue for a lot of people so if everyone could just make the effort . . . "

I'm not sure if this sounds familiar to you, but this is exactly what I was used to dealing with. The vague statements and never really being sure if you were the guilty party or not unless someone was kind enough to shoot you a dirty look. This, however, did not fly for our CEO. She says, "I want to know who specifically is not filling out the forms correctly."

Imagine, if you will, the HR manager turning various shades of red clearly not wanting to throw anyone under the bus. Awkward silence. "Name names," says our CEO.

At this point I feel so bad for this woman and can't help but wonder what type of place I've just agreed to work at (granted I'm sure a lot of people were having similar thoughts about me). She manages to squeak out a name or two. Jane sighs and says, "See it wasn't that bad!" Not sure if I was in agreement at that point. She went on to say that it's not about getting people in trouble but identifying those that are still having the issue so that we make sure we can properly fix it with them.

Now I'm thinking, "Oh, that makes sense when you put it like that."

You may be wondering what these examples have to do with the Wood's Way and, to be honest, it took me some time to be able to connect the dots myself. The Wood's Way is about being truthful, direct, and kind—principles that seem easy enough in theory, but that we all have struggles with putting consistently into practice when we let dysfunctional politeness get in the way.

In regards to my pregnancy story, the Wood's Way is different in that Wood's Homes does not just let their staff wander blindly. The entire management team works to cover each other and each program to ensure that the agency as a whole continues to run smoothly. That, too, may seem like common sense, but I have never worked in a place that strives to run effectively on all cylinders at all times. My past experience was about putting patches on things until they magically got better—or worse. Wood's Homes strives for a team environment so that everyone has the opportunity to provide input on what can be done to run the agency. No one person is better than the next.

As a team, we have to be clear about what it is we are saying and doing with each other and the children and families we support. The thought is, if we can't work that way with each other, then how are we supposed to work with families and children struggling with many difficulties in a way that is effective? Being transparent forces us to behave in a way that's truthful, direct, and kind to everyone. That, I think, is the Wood's Way.

—Audra

91

I would never have recognized her—it was the early 1990s when I hired her. She said she wanted to thank me for something I had taught her that she remembered ever since. I asked if it was a good story or bad. She said, "Good," and as soon as she started I remembered.

Julie had been one of four individuals single-staffed on a night shift at the Bowness Campus when a group of boys showed up at the Phoenix Program with a gun wanting keys to the van and petty cash. These boys (about seven of them) had escaped from Strathmore, where there was, at that time, an open-custody facility. They stole a truck that had a gun in it and drove around for hours until they noticed they were running out of gas.

One of the boys had once lived at the Bowness Campus. He said, "There's a van at Wood's and I know where they keep the key." They drove to the campus and knocked on the door of the Phoenix Program. It was well after midnight.

There are four cottages on the Bowness Campus, and the campus itself is tucked away at the end of a street. At night, one individual is supervising each program and these staff often communicate with each other during the night hours—to borrow sugar and cleaning supplies and the like. So, a knock on the door was not unusual. The female staff, Julie, went to the door and opened it. The boys levelled the gun at her and demanded the key. She said, "I don't have it. Another program has it, I will have to call." This was not true.

They said, "Okay," and let her call. She did, and said to the person on the phone, "There are seven boys here with a gun, and they want the keys to the van."

The boys laughed—and of course the other person called the police, who arrived quickly.

The boys ran to Bowness Park and into nearby backyards, but the police caught them all.

Of course, even though everyone was safe, the staff behaved so well in this crisis, and things turned out in the end, the staff—and especially Julie—were understandably worried and anxious. Julie recalls crying and shaking and not wanting to come back to work that night. She says I was firm about, "needing to get back on the horse." Funny how you don't remember those conversations or ever know if they had an impact (like with the kids) until they come back to you from the other person involved.

What happened after this was also interesting. One of the neighbours called the CEO to complain about the noise the night before and also complained about how wild our kids were. Jane said politely, "Thanks for calling but they were not our kids. Those young men were the ones who escaped from Strathmore. They came to steal a car from us and threatened our staff. It was all very scary for them."

The neighbour was completely silent and then she said, "I never thought it would be you folks who were the victim. I am sorry for jumping to conclusions."

After that, we joined the Neighbourhood Block Watch even though our neighbours gasped at the thought at first. We proved that we could be a great neighbour in our community, as we are terrific in a crisis, calm and level-headed, and also we are up all night!

—Sandra Snape

92

I had been working in the oil and gas industry for years. My job was one of those lovely well-paying jobs—you could come and go as you pleased. But it became a clock-watching job. At one point it struck me that it didn't excite me to go to work; I was just waiting to go home.

My sister-in-law worked at Mount Royal University, in criminology. Part of her course was child and youth care. And I thought about it and realized, "Oh man, I'm going back to school at my age—thirty something."

So, I went back and got my diploma. When it came time to do my practicum, I was very curious about community re-entry. But shortly after I started, the funding for community re-entry was cut. And so, kind of without it being my focus, I found myself at the Phoenix Program, the program for teen sex offenders. Peter Wittig was my supervisor. It was a whole other ball of wax. What you learned from books was not at all what you needed.

I didn't know that it would become a long-term career. I just got hooked. Partially because Wood's Homes is a relationship-based organization, and a highly ethical organization, and that all fit with me. The Phoenix Program became my baby for a long time.

Then I moved over to Director Bjorn Johansson's Habitat Program, working in domestic violence. You've got boys in the program whose every response to almost anything is violence. They come in and smash the bejesus out of each other and the program itself. They were terrifically hierarchical. Kids immediately ranked the new person.

Then I worked in foster care. It was a big change from residential. It was about defining the difference between crisis and residential. Then I was asked by Director Teri Basi to be program manager of Phoenix—and realized that this was my niche. I look at these kids and the trauma they have experienced, and wonder how they have survived. The more I understood and learned, the more I was able to separate boys from their behaviours.

That was just about six years ago. Since then, I've managed the Eagle Moon Lodge. I managed Phoenix. And I manage Catalyst. Someone must think I have something to give to these programs.

This journey took me back to when I started. I still value Wood's Homes as being very different in terms of how we work with kids and families. Unless we have relationships established, change is not going to happen. I love that we do not have locked rooms, or locked facilities. That goes against our values. We never say no; we never give up; we never turn anyone away.

I'm often astounded when I think of the Phoenix kids. They have been for the most part victimized themselves. I'm always so impressed and surprised at the level of risk they take, by simply admitting that they have done something pretty horrific, and speak to what they did and share some tragic troubling details about it, and then work through it. And being held accountable. Especially when, often, their abusers have not been held accountable.

That's true of all of our kids who have survived in communities that are troubled, and often where abuse is rampant. The best we can do is teach them new skills.

We have high expectations of these kids. The day they leave and the graduation is held, the kids are crying out of happiness, and success. And the staff are in tears, too, because the relationship is that strong.

—Joyce Macdonald

93

This midnight shift seemed unusually dark and cloudy and the Lethbridge shelter was all but full. This night was—to say the least—not your ordinary midnight shift. Usually this would be a time for paperwork, cleaning, and the computer. For some reason this was not to be, as youth were up and down, and staff were running to keep the unit quiet for those who were trying to stay settled.

As the night wore on and the efforts of the staff to maintain peace and quiet began to pay off, the bell rang, and one of our female staff went to the door. At the door stood an older adult male, motioning for her to let him in. In her wisdom, she did not and tried to communicate with him through the glass door. As this went on it became frustrating for both parties, so she decided to open the door so she could be clear in her answers to the man.

When the door opened, suddenly he exposed a baseball bat and beer bottle and began to threaten the staff. Her reflexes saved her. She was able to close the door and bolt the lock before her would-be attacker could make his move. She immediately went to the phone to call the police. The would-be attacker could see this and left the area. The proper steps were followed to keep the youth and the unit safe and secure.

This type of situation isn't supposed to happen here in our small city—but what an example of what could happen and what an eye opener to the dangers that lurk around every corner in every town or city, no matter the size or location.

94

Aldo attended the George Wood Learning Centre, a school for kids who live in one of the residential programs on Bowness Campus. The staff and teachers very quickly discovered that he had not been in school since he was twelve and was academically behind by at least six grade levels. Aldo spent the first three months either not attending the school or coming to school in the morning and being so disruptive and violent that there was no possibility that he could complete a full day of school. Staff spent substantial time with Aldo, trying to engage him and find that carrot that would inspire him to learn and want to be at school. The carrot, to our disbelief, was acting.

The staff were working with the students to put on their annual Christmas play when, out of the blue, Aldo became engaged and wanted to be involved. Aldo took on the role of scriptwriter and supporting director, and his passion came through. To our disbelief, he attended school every day and made sure his behaviour was good enough so he could take part in the show.

The play was a huge success, and Aldo continued his commitment to learning. Aldo left Wood's Homes and went into a community school and at the age of nineteen, graduated.

95

It was 1989, before anyone even spoke the words *walk-in* or *single session* in a psychotherapeutic context. Dr. Philip Perry (former CEO, Wood's Homes) had heard about a program called the Minneapolis Walk-In Counseling Center—a place that had been operating successfully for about two decades. He began to try to convince people that this model should be implemented in Calgary.

Research indicated that the most improvement in therapy happens in the first sessions, and he challenged anyone who gave him a counterargument. Traditional groups of clinicians (including those at Wood's Homes) were not easily convinced.

However, Dr. Perry (now retired) and Dr. Arnie Slive (who was Wood's Homes clinical director for many years but who now practises in Texas) set out to persuade the community. The idea was to provide a walk-in clinic, an immediate, accessible, affordable service for children, youth, and families in northeast Calgary where services were scarce.

It was an uphill battle convincing the reluctant and the suspicious. Professionals across all disciplines were critical and unbelieving of its possibilities. Eventually a task force was created and then an advisory committee, made up of citizens from education, police, mental health and other organizations, and corporate leaders.

The committee helped choose the Eastside name; established the principles of immediate, accessible, affordable; helped find the location; set the hours of the clinic (based on what they felt their communities needed); and established relationships with other service providers so that Eastside was seen as a place of mutual benefit. For instance, wait-listed patients from Emergency could be referred directly to Eastside, and Eastside could refer directly to the hospital or partner organization when they were faced with a client requiring immediate assistance.

In the end, the few people who recognized that Eastside would be a service to help with funding scarcity, high demands for services, and unspeakably long wait lists, won out. A cadre of advocates grew in numbers as the multiple benefits were realized.

Dr. Perry and Dr. Slive continued to work the community, advertising, going on a kind of road show to describe the service being offered and how it could help people. It didn't take long for word of the service to spread and, soon enough, the service was launched with funding from Wood's Homes, Alberta Mental Health, and private donations. Eastside Family Centre was launched in January 1990.

What started off as a great notion is now a successful counselling service that is replicated in other centres across Canada. Eastside Family Centre is a place that offers walk-in, single-session counselling at no charge.

96

This isn't a story about a client of Wood's, but rather about a staff person who grew up at Wood's.

I started at Wood's when I was thirty-nine—not really a kid, but I'd been at a previous job for over fifteen years, so I was young in different working experiences. I worked my way up from an accounting clerk to the supervisor of Wood's in a period of four years. I remained in this role for another six and a half years. In May of 2009 I left Wood's Homes for a lot of reasons, one of which was that I felt I needed to make sure I could still learn something new. A drastic step, but one I felt I had to take.

I was gone for three years and three months, almost to the day. Why did I return? It was at the AGM in 2012 when I heard about all the good things Wood's Homes was involved in. I said to myself, "I really can't keep coming back to hear about this stuff and know that I'm not part of such a rich diverse organization." So I made the decision that I wouldn't return to any more AGMs if I wasn't working there.

Who would have thought a mere month later there would be a job opening in the Finance Department? After an interview, I was accepted back into the Wood's family to continue my journey.

I am in good company as a Comeback Kid. There have been many before me, and I am sure there will be many who will follow. We all work here for a myriad of reasons, but one thing is certain: once you have worked at Wood's you will never forget your time here. It will be a part of your makeup.

—Pat Keppler

97

When I arrived at the University of Calgary it was about 1978. That's when I first encountered Wood's Homes, because I was the instructor in the Faculty of Social Work responsible for field placement students.

Wood's Homes back then was viewed as a very reliable setting for these placements. The people at Wood's would say to me, "If you have a student who is interested in working with troubled youth, we'll take them." Other places wanted to interview the student first, but Wood's Homes was interested in taking on any student who was eager to learn.

Flash forward many years later at the University of Calgary. The relationship between institutions had become more formal. We'd developed agreements with agencies about placements. Wood's Homes was at the forefront of the philosophy that if they were our student, they had a placement with Wood's. That began a special relationship between Wood's Homes and the Faculty of Social Work. We started to view Wood's as a real partner in the Social Work endeavours.

Wood's Homes established the Wood's Homes bursary in 1996 for working with youth. Now they not only provided placements but they provided financial support. This set an example for other agencies. It established a real relationship of interdependence with the university. Wood's relied upon the university to train students; we relied upon them for professional placements. They relied upon us to generate researchers; they set the context.

This set the standard for all the others who came along after: the YW, and all the other social agencies who then provided bursaries for students.

It's all part of the care that Wood's has for educating social workers—you always hold your field placements close to your heart.

We have had instances of students having to quit their program due to financial stress. The university couldn't find the resources, and Wood's Homes would lend them money. They have a discretionary fund that permits them to be nimble. If it were the difference between having the student drop out or graduate, Wood's Homes would lend them the money. And again, it's all part of a philosophy that embraces their entire operations: not giving up on people.

—Gayla Rogers

98

It was well after quitting time, and I was in my office. Located at the Parkdale Campus (in the current Tuer Children's Mental Health Centre), my office was close to the lunchroom.

All the other staff had long gone home. The only sound was the humming of the old refrigerator and the sniffles of a boy. I could hear the counsellor consoling him. Their work must be difficult and complicated, I thought. After a few minutes I became curious and found a reason to stroll by the room. And there he was—a client with whom I was fairly familiar.

You see, he used to steal the candy in my office, which sat right next to where Dr. Harris, a psychiatrist, regularly consulted with our young clients. One day I thought it would be nice to have a dish of candies to offer clients as they waited for Dr. Harris in the hallway—my door was always open and, if they felt like it, I shared idle chit-chat with them.

For the most part, the young people politely took one candy at a time, which is the way this teen started. He would take one every time we saw each other. But it didn't take long for him to ask for two, then three, and then eventually one day came the question: "Can I take the whole jar?"

I said, "No. If you did that, there wouldn't be any candies for the others."

He walked away in a huff. A few days later, I came to my desk and found my glass candy jar broken into pieces! And I knew who the culprit was. The next time I saw him, I asked him why he'd done that and he simply shrugged.

I never put candy out again. Lessons learned. But despite his "mistake," I sensed this boy had a gentleness tucked way inside. But there are consequences—we all learn that soon enough.

Back to the lunchroom, where I heard him slowly unfolding, oblivious to any audience outside of his counsellor. It was time for him to return home. Staff had held a goodbye party for him—he was so impressed with that. He had been the centre of attention and he liked it, but feared he never would be again. And he was sad. This was the only place he'd known for the past three years. He was afraid to let go of us.

It's then that I realized the effect Wood's Homes has on its clients. For many, it's the first time they've encountered people who actually care. People who worry, who think about them, people who take notice and miss them when they are not where they're supposed to be. Wood's knew he was ready for the outside world and, despite his protest, they believed in his ability to make it in the world, on his own.

And they were right.

—Sylvia MacIver

99

I became the chief executive officer for the Boys and Girls Club in 1988. One of my first points of business was to hold a meeting with Jane. I knew after that first day and that two-hour lunch that I would be spending the next years seeking advice and resources from Wood's Homes—and I did just that for fifteen years.

After four years as CEO, the board changed, and I experienced some issues. Once again I sought Jane's assistance. She didn't just have a casual lunch with me, she spoke with board member Doug Rogan, and they developed advice and strategy for me. This was an individual and an agency believing they could support other agencies. That spoke so well of them.

Since then we have partnered on a number of other projects, and I knew that the partnerships would prove beneficial. Some organizations don't like to do that—but Wood's does. It's been amazing.

They went through an accreditation process and invited me to be part of the community feedback group. I was blown away by the transparency they demonstrated. I sat there with the accreditors learning and offering my opinions. How can we all understand from near misses and make sure they never happen again? I am continually impressed by their transparency and leadership.

—Cheryl Doherty

100

To get to be a hundred years old, you have to grow and change with society. And Wood's Homes probably managed that by keeping its eye on the main thing. George Wood was moved to found an orphanage by feelings of care and compassion—not just a notion of becoming a childcare agency. And some places are good at being that. I think we are good at being ambitious and keeping kids at the heart of the matter.

Those familiar stories keep getting repeated. In the end it's the same old, same old. As much as you think it is a different world, a hundred years later it's the same kids, the same situations.

In 1926 George Wood came to town. He had ambition. He left one place, came to another, accepted too many kids. He got a manor in

Bowness, and he begged the societies for funding. During all that time, the doors of Wood's never closed.

For over one hundred years, we've offered good care. Maybe he had the right idea: he was old, he didn't believe in doing anything fancy.

Just do the right thing.

—Susan Gardiner

The Orphanage Gates

Reverend George Wood first passed through the gates of the Hextal Estate in 1928 in search of a new home for the growing number of orphaned children in his care. To many of the thousands of children who have lived here these gates hold special memories. Though the alignment of this entrance has changed and the gates' role is now symbolic they remain as sentinels over daily activities at Wood's Homes.

Years ago, the Janett Family of Bowness saved these gates from the scrap yard. This family recognized their historical and emotional significance to Bowness as well as their distinctive Old English wrought iron design. In the summer of 1997 the Janett Family kindly donated these gates back to Wood's Homes on the condition that they never again be removed from these pillars.

Plaque next to Wood's Home entrance to the Bowness Campus.

Acknowledgements

So many people should be thanked for their efforts into making this book happen. First and foremost would be the Reverend Wood. Had he not initially accepted those first children, there would be no Wood's Homes, nor a hundredth anniversary to celebrate. That debt of gratitude extends much further, however. All those who submitted their written stories, or told me their stories, and those who pointed me in directions where I was likely to find stories. Those presently serving in administrative capacities at Wood's and those who have served in the past, who helped to create a powerful culture of caring and were willing to share their successes and failures with me. The members of the orphan's alumnae organization, the Homers, who were incredibly generous with their time. The many, many individuals who submitted wonderful stories that could not be included in as finite and limiting a structure as one hundred stories. Many thanks to all of you. The Calgary Foundation must also be acknowledged for the generous financial support it offered, without which this publication could never have happened.

Clem Martini
November 2013

101 – A BONUS STORY

When I first came here, I was looking for belonging. I'd worked in other agencies, and you didn't feel like you belonged or were heard. I liked that we said yes. I've learned to appreciate that there are kids in this world that nobody wants.

I got a call from a social worker up in Nunavut, once. He said, "I've called everyone in Canada and nobody will help me."

I said, "I'm going to help you."

He said, "You don't even know what the trouble is yet."

I said, "It doesn't matter. I know you have a child who is in trouble, and I'm going to help you."

It turns out that this child had shot himself in the neck. He was in a hospital.

I said, "Get him fixed. Put him on a plane. We'll take him."

I don't want to be part of a world that says no to kids. If a kid is in trouble, and needs help, the philosophy has got to be that we'll say, "Yes."

—Teri Basi

Entrance to the orphanage, with gates.

Appendix A:
Wood's Homes Timeline of Events

1914

(Conflicting entries exist for this initial date, some of which are as late as 1915.)

Reverend George Wood is stopped by a soldier in Innisfail, Alberta, who asks him if he would look after his two motherless children as he is headed to service overseas. Reverend Wood, who had also lost his wife, says yes. Sadly, the soldier does not return, but that pivotal moment is the foundation for Wood's Christian Homes.

1916

Reverend Wood proposes to Annie Jarvie, a social worker, fellow Scot, and family friend. He proposes by telegram as she is climbing the gangplank of a steamer at Montreal. Annie says yes and soon after takes on the role of Mother Wood.

1918

Now with other children in their care, the Woods relocate to Olds. This, after moving three times in Innisfail in search of increasingly larger homes.

1921

May 7 marks the incorporation of the board of directors of Wood's Christian Homes.

1926

The Woods, with thirty-two children in tow, move into the Hextall Estate in Bowness (which at the time was available for a fraction of its original cost). The property was $65,000 and secured with $18,000 (without interest) using Reverend Wood's insurance policy as collateral.

1928

Reverend Wood dies November 27, following a short illness. Records show that years of unceasing strain and anxiety had taken their toll.

1929

Mother Wood takes over the home. Mrs. Wood is the matron; Mr. David B. Robertson is business manager. As the number of children increases, house-parents and cooks are hired to complement a very small staff group. (An average of one hundred children live at the home at any given time.) The board of trustees is headed by Mr. W. Snaddon.

1939

Mother Wood dies November 4, after a number of years of poor health. Her successor is Mrs. Agnes Longair.

1943–1948

Mrs. Longair retires and is replaced by Mrs. J. Nicholson, Mrs. E. Hutchson, and, finally, Mrs. L. Blackador.

1953

Mr. A. Bartle, the school superintendent for more than twenty-five years, dies.

1954

Mr. David Robertson retires after twenty-six years. Mr. and Mrs. Arthur Jeal joined the home as manager and matron.

1956

A new manager's residence is built on the Bowness site.

1957

Mrs. Jeal resigns (succeeded by Mrs. Birch); Mr. Jeal becomes the new superintendent.

1958

One cottage is built on the site, with the intent of holding twenty-four children and two staff members. This cottage (which today houses the Phoenix Program) is called the Robertson Cottage.

1961

A social work department is established at Wood's Homes.

1965

As part of the fiftieth anniversary project, three cottages are built on the site. By this time, about half of the children have come to the home privately, the other half from city or provincial agencies.

1969

The home closes to re-evaluate its role in child welfare work and the twenty-nine children who are there move to other homes. This is largely due to changes in government process. The board makes a study of the areas of greatest need in child care in Calgary and again decides on serving troubled children.

1970

Wood's Home reopens, operating under the Department of Health. Staff include a nurse, social worker, psychologist, child psychiatrist, and their assistants and are employed by the University of Calgary and Wood's Christian Homes.

1972

A whole-family treatment model is initiated for a short period of time (two years) in the newly created cottages. Then a parented group-home model replaces this. Carol Ann Probert is the executive director.

1982

The Adolescent Care Centre (in planning stages since 1974) is constructed on government land in Parkland and opens in March. It, along with the Bowness Campus programs and Hillhurst group home, is now the responsibility of Dr. Brian Plowman, executive director and a psychiatrist.

1983

A major grounds redevelopment project is undertaken on the Bowness Campus, jointly funded by the federal and provincial governments and Wood's Homes. This project includes the construction of a trail through the Douglas fir forest on the western portion of Wood's Homes' forty-one-acre property. Today it is designated as a provincial heritage site.

1984

Dr. Plowman returns to private practice. Dr. Philip Perry becomes the new executive director of Wood's Homes.

1984–1988

Bowness residential buildings are completely renovated and many improvements are made to the office and school buildings. Wood's Homes first fundraiser is hired.

1986

Services start to be offered by Wood's Homes in Lethbridge and Red Deer.

1988

The board of directors of Wood's Homes becomes increasingly concerned over the needs of many neglected and abused children, as government funding becomes more restricted. The board moves to raise Wood's Homes' profile as a charitable organization.

1995

Dr. Perry leaves to work on Vancouver Island. Jane Matheson becomes the executive director and eventually the CEO.

1997

The first capital campaign in more than forty years begins. Schools are renovated on both sites.

2000

The Wood's Homes Foundation is created. Bill Roberts, previously director of finance, becomes the executive director.

2003

A second capital campaign begins.

2005

After years of homelessness and less than adequate dwellings, EXIT's new house is created in partnership with Central United Church. One million dollars is raised for renovations of the Canadian Bible Society building on 7th Avenue (downtown Calgary) in exchange for ten years of free rent.

2007

Wood's Christian Homes becomes Wood's Homes, as it identifies as a non-denominational organization that serves all faiths.

2008

Construction and renovations begin on the Parkdale Campus. A new administration building, a playground area, and improved grounds, as well as the Tuer Children's Mental Health Centre are developed.

2012

Construction begins on the renewal of the Bowness Campus with the construction of the Hextall Building and added outdoor recreational activity space. The project is scheduled for completion in 2014—Wood's one-hundredth anniversary.

2013

The new Hextall Building opens in November.

2014

The new Family Centre on the Bowness Campus will open in the summer.

Appendix B:
Wood's Homes Programs as Developed
Through the Decades

1950
Bowness
Wood's Homes has four residential programs and the Hextall Building ("the big house").

1954
Bowness Campus School
Wood's Homes and the Calgary Board of Education launch a partnership to provide specialized education and mental health treatment services on the Bowness Campus.

1973
Hillhurst
A house in the Hillhurst community is purchased to provide care for six to eight adolescents transitioning to adulthood.

1982
Parkdale Campus
The Adolescent Care Centre now includes residential treatment programs and a school.

1985
Permanent Care (Evergreen today)
This program has gone through numerous evolutions since its start. It serves troubled young people who display violence and substance abuse with a history of placement breakdowns.

Exceptional Needs
Developed to meet the needs of youth (twelve to eighteen) experiencing multiple biological, psychological, social, and mental health challenges, this program demonstrates a need for a service that is a step up from traditional outpatient community-based services, and a step down from intensive hospital-based services.

Family Focus
Works to engage and unite families who are struggling with various types of problems.

Stabilization

Unique in its time, this program offers immediate help to families in crisis situations by providing a short-term stay, allowing young people and their guardians, parents, and/or caregivers a timeout of three to five days. It offers opportunity for all to stabilize and assess next steps to find solutions.

1986

Parkland Clinical Treatment Centre

A continuum of services including Stabilization, Family Focus, and Exceptional Needs. Based in Red Deer, it is intended for young people and their families residing in central Alberta. In 1997, this program evolved into a separate legal society and an autonomous, community-driven organization now called Parkland Youth Homes.

Community Living Network/Lethbridge

Our therapeutic foster care services begin in Lethbridge. They include Aboriginal foster homes on the Kainai Reserve and across southern Alberta.

1987

Community Resource Team (CRT)

CRT is a 24/7 phone and mobile crisis response service that provides immediate crisis intervention phone services to families at risk of breaking down.

Family Restoration Program

A short-term program focusing on restoring family harmony.

1989

EXIT Community Outreach

A storefront in downtown Calgary, it provides basic needs as well as skills and hope for the future to homeless youth (twelve to twenty-four) and/or young people at risk of sexual exploitation.

Eastside Family Centre

The brainchild of Dr. Arnie Slive and Dr. Philip Perry, Eastside is the first resource of its kind in Canada, providing a community-based, walk-in, single-session model of mental health service delivery that was affordable, accessible, and immediate.

Northern Network of Services (NNS)
The NNS is located in Whitehorse, Yukon Territory, for about six years. It was a residential program with stabilization, family focus, and exceptional needs components for thirteen- to seventeen-year-old youth and their families who lived throughout the YT. In 1994, the program was taken over by a community board but ended two years later.

1990

Caregiver Network
A collection of three foster homes in the northwest of Calgary that assisted with youth transitioning from residential services.

Phoenix (formerly Community Resource Centre, CRC)
CRC was an open-custody program for young people from the Calgary Young Offenders Centre. Phoenix developed over time from the CRC program, focusing on sexually intrusive behaviours of young men. Dr. Philip Perry, former CEO of Wood's Homes, started Phoenix, as it seemed young people with sexual development issues were being ignored.

1990–1996

Satellite school programs
Wood's Homes delivers a series of satellite school programs for work experience. They include Discovering Choices, New Directions, and Turning Points.

1991

Canadiana Centre
Canadiana is a four-part addictions program operating as a fee-for-service facility for Alberta youth and their families. Canadiana was in partnership with the business community of Calgary, operating for three years without government funding (mostly through private donations). A'sokina evolved from Canadiana, and was a solvent-abuse program supported by a contribution agreement from Ottawa. This fee-for-service for substance-abuse treatment program remained First Nations–based for over four years.

EXIT van
Launched as a complement to services provided at EXIT Community Outreach, the van has provided mobile outreach services for many years to youth downtown at night. Today, the van visits disadvantaged communities and offers onsite counselling, referral, and food.

1992
Altadore
Wood's Homes starts a home in this community called Summit Lodge for girls struggling with solvent addiction and sexual abuse. In 1997, Altadore starts as a transition to adulthood service for males and females twelve to seventeen.

1995
Eagle Moon Lodge
Derived from the Canadiana Centre, Eagle Moon Lodge (which at one time was Lone Pipe Lodge, then Summit Lodge) launches in 1995 as its own distinct fee-for-service program.

1997
Foster Care Network
A tender for standard foster care becomes available and Wood's Homes applies for it in order to solidify a continuum of care for the children, youth, and families that they serve.

Habitat
A residential program for boys who have witnessed family violence, this program incorporates family work as well. The program won a Dare to Dream Award in 1999.

1999
Catalyst
A residential program for young people with complex mental health issues.

EXIT Youth Shelter (Calgary)
EXIT provides shelter to young people (twelve to seventeen) who are in conflict with their parents, away from home or homeless, or who have left their Child Welfare placement.

2001

The Home Connections Program

The Home Connections program offers a more convenient way to serve clients who are unable to come to Wood's Homes. It works with all family members, in the home, school, or community. In Canmore, there is a satellite program.

Our Lady of Lourdes

A day treatment service first offered at St. Anthony School. In 2005, the program moves to its current location with the new name, Our Lady of Lourdes.

Over the past few years this program expanded to include eight community classrooms that support both the educational and treatment needs of students from across the city. This program ended in 2013.

Research Department

This department begins with the funding of one person in 2001. By doing this, Wood's Homes put measuring program and client outcomes front and centre to its work. This focus has grown over the past decade.

2002

Home Connections/Lethbridge

This program is a combination of Family Preservation and Youth Mentoring. Family Preservation is in-home support given to families with high needs, and Youth Mentoring is provided for youth (up to eighteen).

2003

Collingwood/14th Street

The Collingwood/14th Street Program is a supported, parented home with more supervision than a foster-care setting provides. Youth are taught how to live independently and successfully in the community.

Emergency Youth Shelter/Lethbridge

This service begins after a youth shelter committee is formed following a community forum on homelessness. The shelter is modeled after the EXIT Youth Shelter in Calgary.

ROMP
The Recreational Opportunities Mentorship Program (ROMP) develops from a recreational committee called ACORN that recognizes the benefits of outdoor experiences for troubled youth.

New Outlook
A program in partnership with VRRI (now Vecova), New Outlook is a transitional program for young adults (eighteen to twenty-four) with complex mental health concerns and a long history with Children's Services and Justice. This program ended in 2012.

2004
Wheatland County/Strathmore
Crisis stabilization, long-term group care, and in-home family support located in Strathmore in two parented and staff-supported homes.

2005
Exceptional Needs Program (U12)
Short-term residential services for very troubled children under twelve, who cannot manage in the community, in a foster home, or at home.

2007
Capitol Hill Stabilization
A residential program for children (six to twelve) in the community of Capitol Hill, it provides a refuge for children who have broken down or are at risk of breaking down, and who are current Child Welfare placements.

2008
Trailcross Treatment Centre, Fort Smith, NWT
Wood's Homes provides therapeutic residential treatment for young people living in the North.

Children's Village School
In a partnership with Calgary Board of Education, Wood's Homes provides the treatment component of learning to elementary students who have displayed difficulty in community school settings.

2009

Family Support Network (OBSD)
A new business model of delivering services to children and families, in conjunction with a Children's Services unit. This system, called Outcomes-Based Service Delivery, places a stronger focus on service results. Wood's Homes is named a lead agency.

Stepping Stones (Fort McMurray)
Wood's Homes is asked by a group of professionals and concerned citizens to help with the young homeless population. Stepping Stones provides temporary shelter and is aimed at helping homeless young people find a way off the streets.

Helios
A second program in partnership with VRRI (now Vecova), Helios is designed as an intensive supportive group home for clients (eighteen to twenty-four) who need twenty-four-hour support to address their mental health needs. This program ended in 2012.

2010

Aftercare Services
The first of its kind in Canada, Aftercare fills a crucial gap in the continued treatment of young people by accompanying them back home to their community (often in remote areas) after being discharged from residential treatment, or orienting young people and their families to upcoming treatment services.

Family Connections (OBSD)
Outcomes-Based Services in Lethbridge, patterned after the Family Support Network (OBSD) in Calgary.

New Horizon
In partnership with Horizon Housing Society and the Calgary Homeless Foundation, New Horizon offers temporary, cost-reduced housing for young people who might otherwise join the adult homeless population.

2012

Roofs for Youth
Launched in partnership with the Calgary John Howard Society and Calgary Young Offenders Centre, this program provides support to youth before and after sentencing.

Culinary Youth Employment Program

In partnership with the Calgary John Howard Society, this program teaches teens how to cook and helps them to prepare for and pursue employment in the culinary field.

Foster Care Expansion

In 2012, Wood's Homes acquires another foster care program and now offers up to 120 foster care beds with fifty-five foster homes across the Calgary community. Our homes now serve a broader age range of infants, children, and youth.

Transportation Services

A busy service that provides delivery for children in care as well as supervised visitation services for families, children, and other agencies.

About the Editor

Clem Martini is an award-winning playwright, novelist, and screen-writer with over thirty plays and ten books of fiction and nonfiction to his credit, including the Calgary Book Award–winning *Bitter Medicine: A Graphic Memoir of Mental Illness*. He has served on the boards of numerous writing organizations including the Alberta Playwrights Network (vice-president), the Playwrights Guild of Canada (president), and the Canadian Creative Writers and Writing Programs (founding president). His texts on play-writing, *The Blunt Playwright* and *The Greek Playwright*, are employed in universities and colleges across the country. From 1998 through 2007, he taught theatre classes to children at Wood's Homes. He is currently a professor in the School of the Creative and Performing Arts at the University of Calgary.